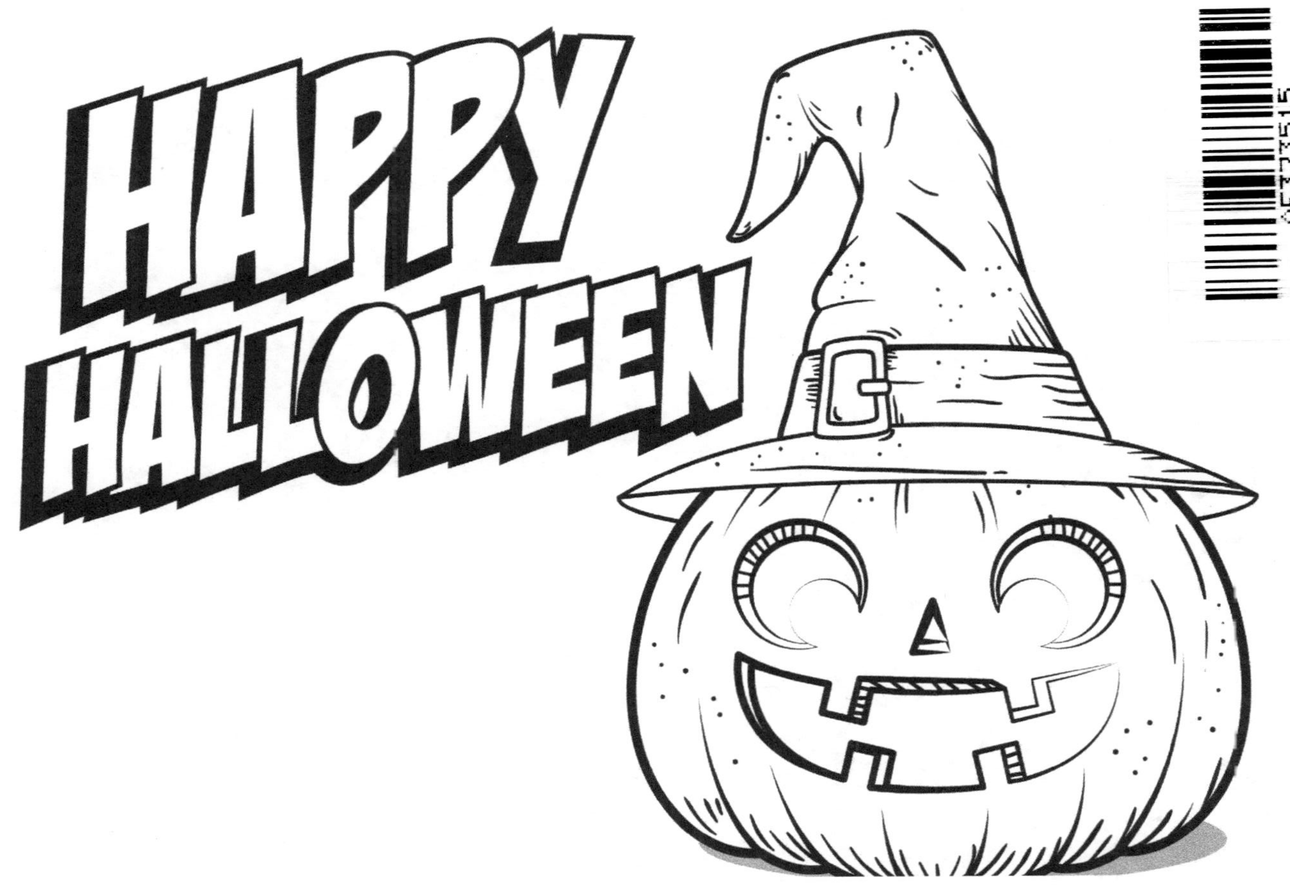

AF373515

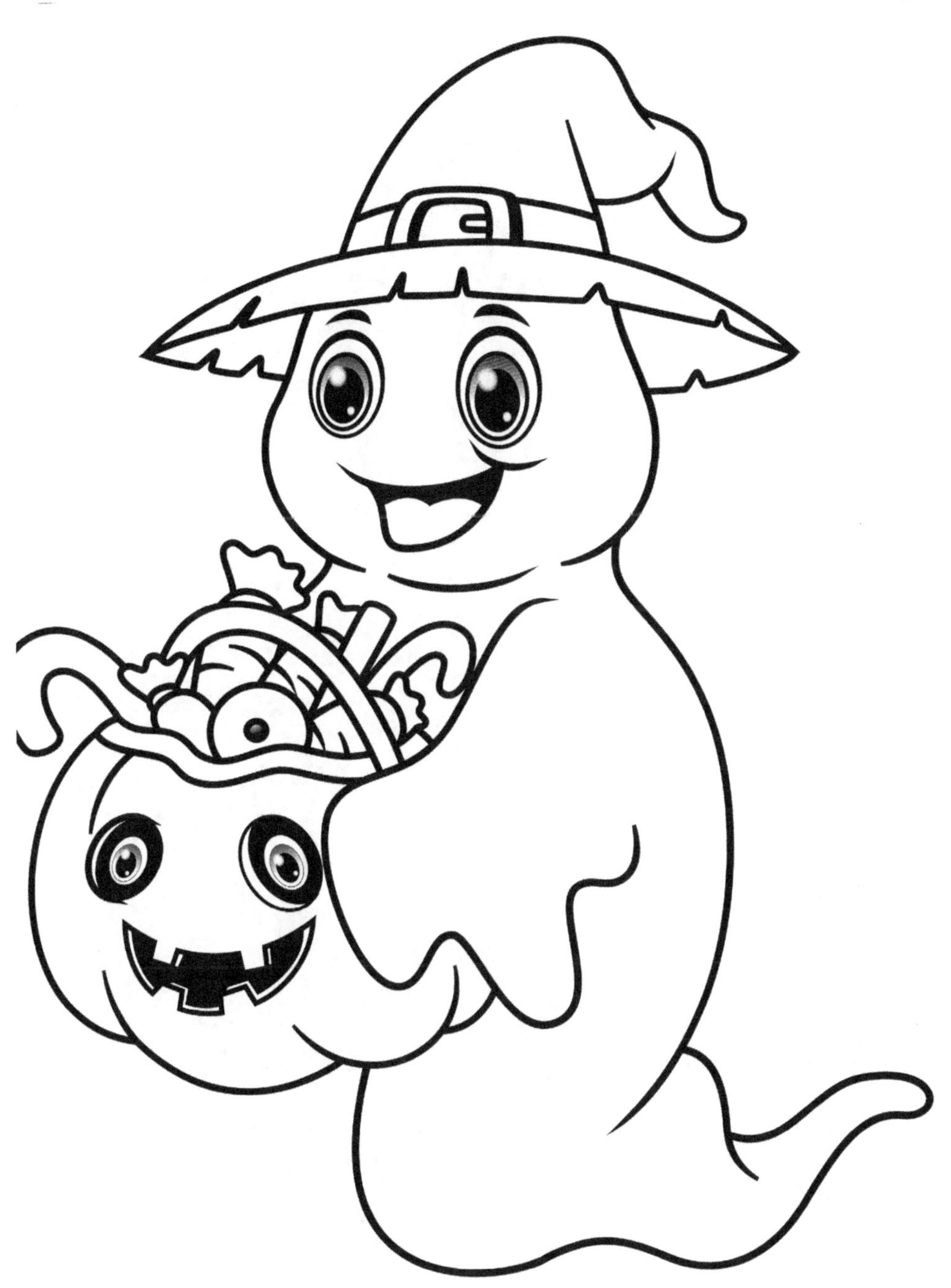

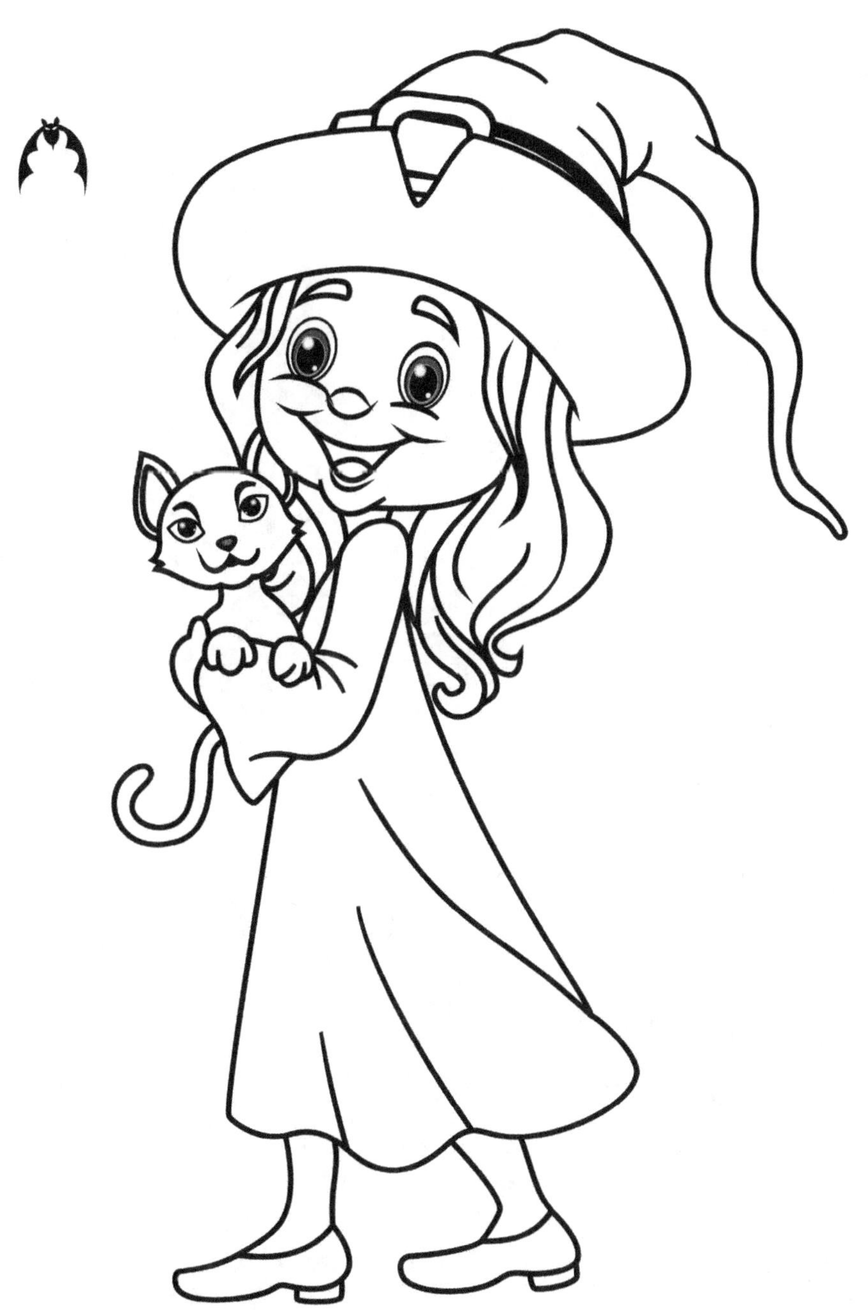

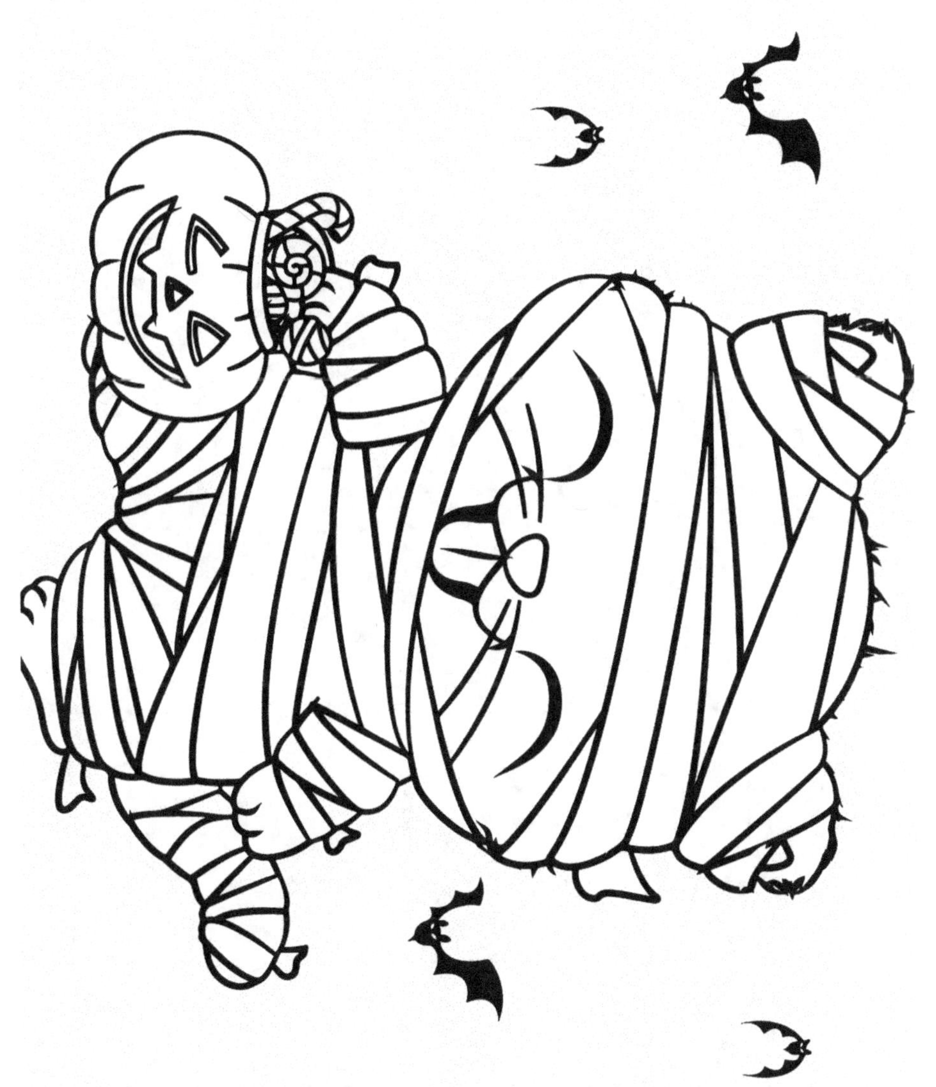

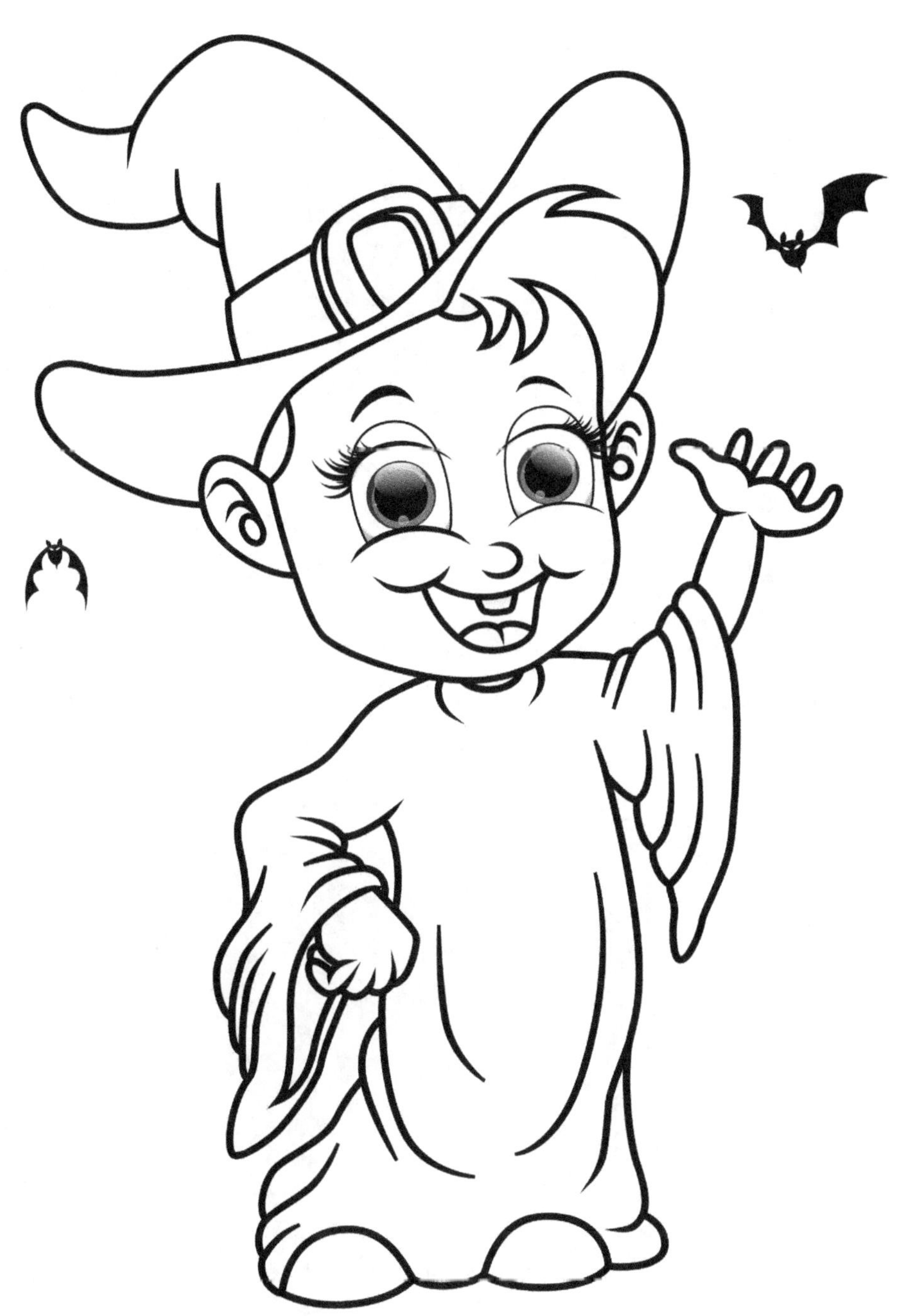

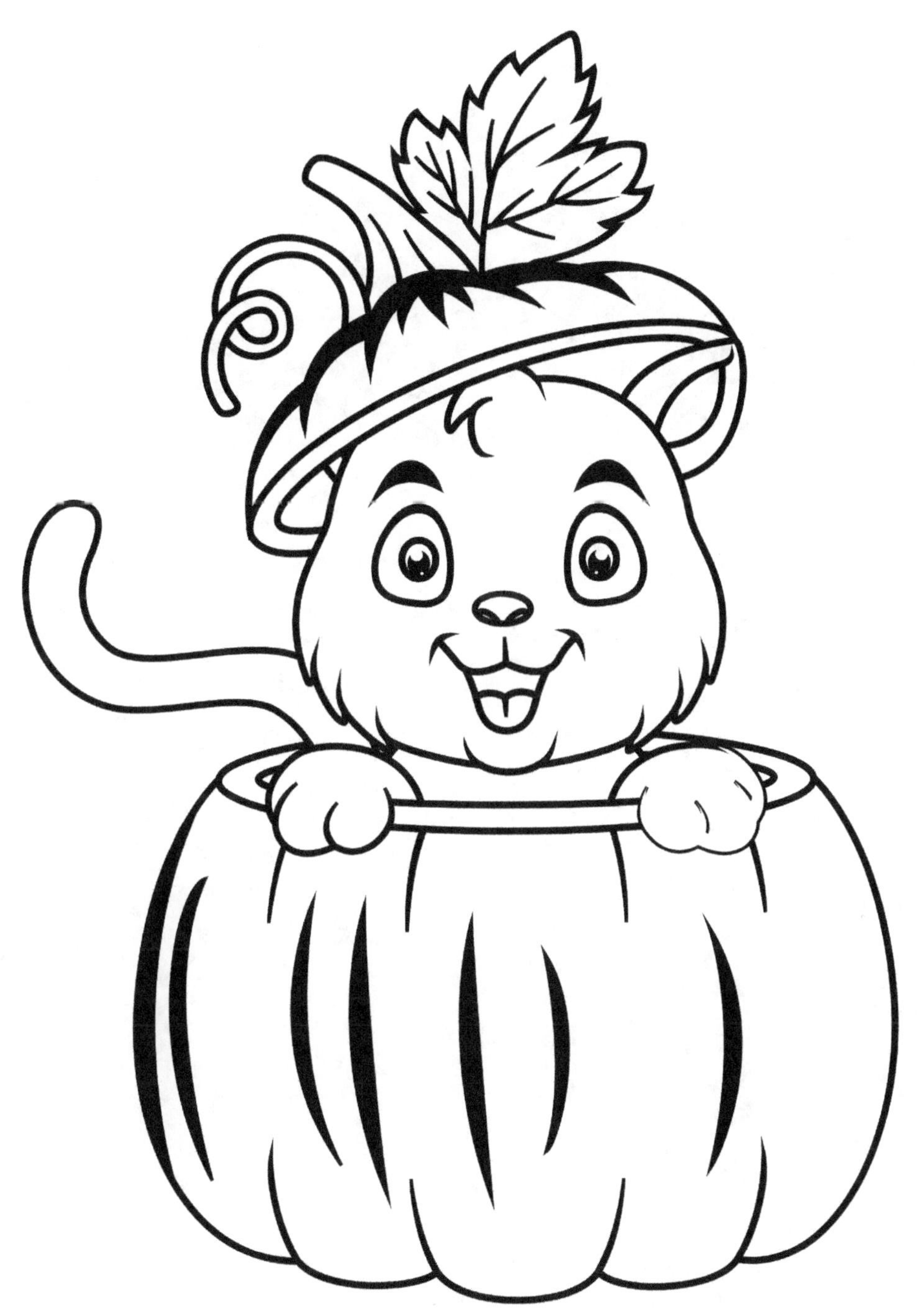

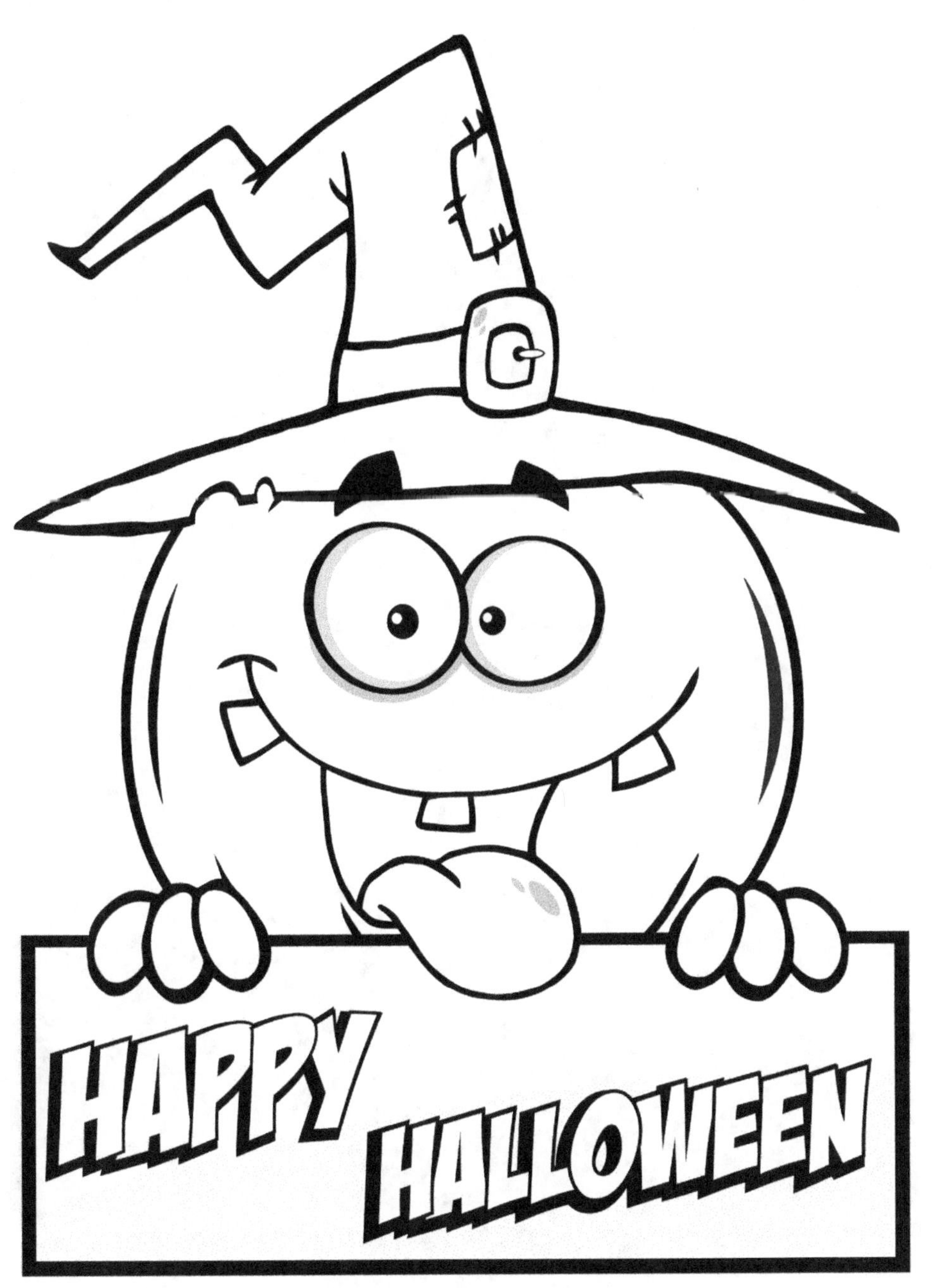

HAPPY
HALLOWEEN

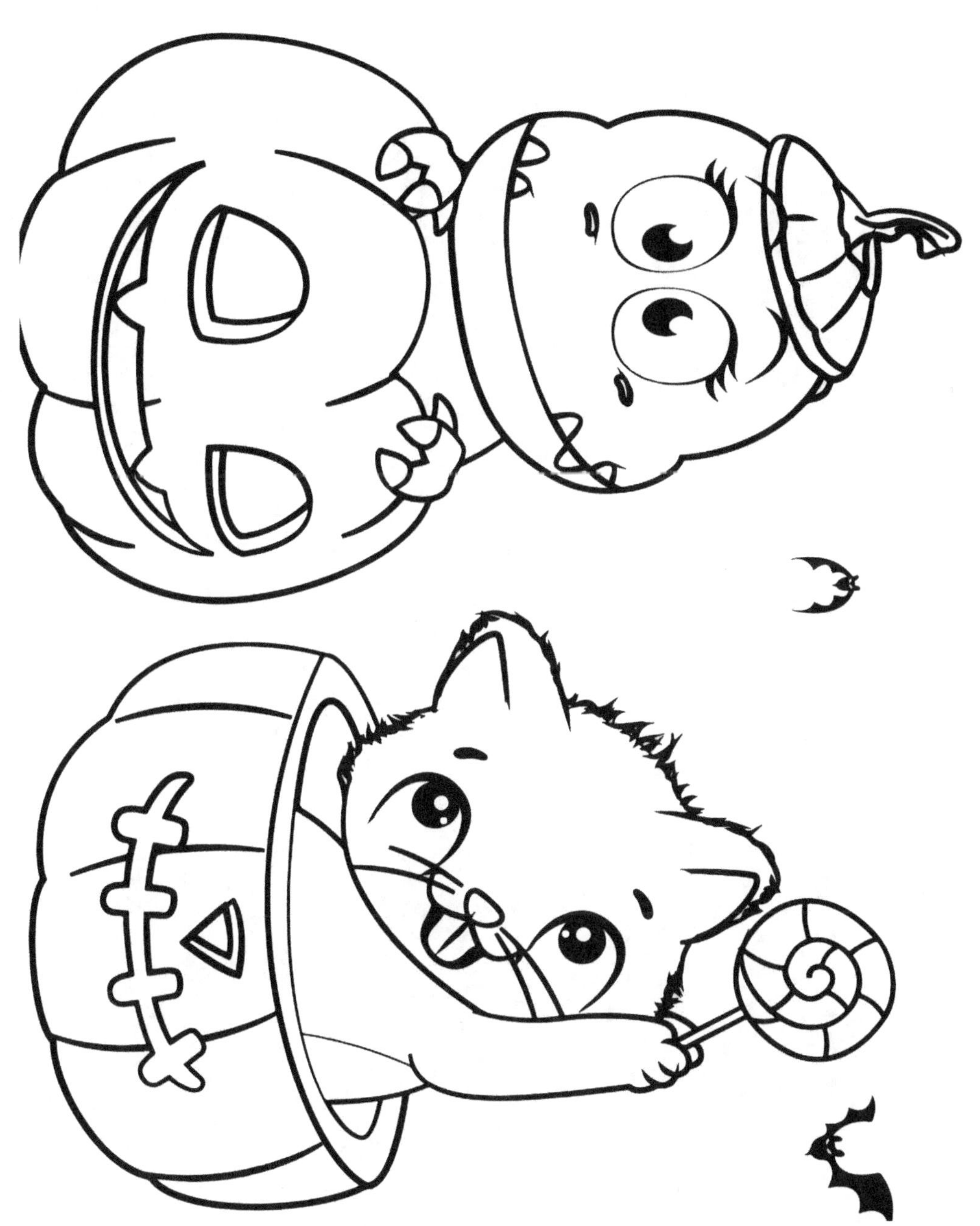

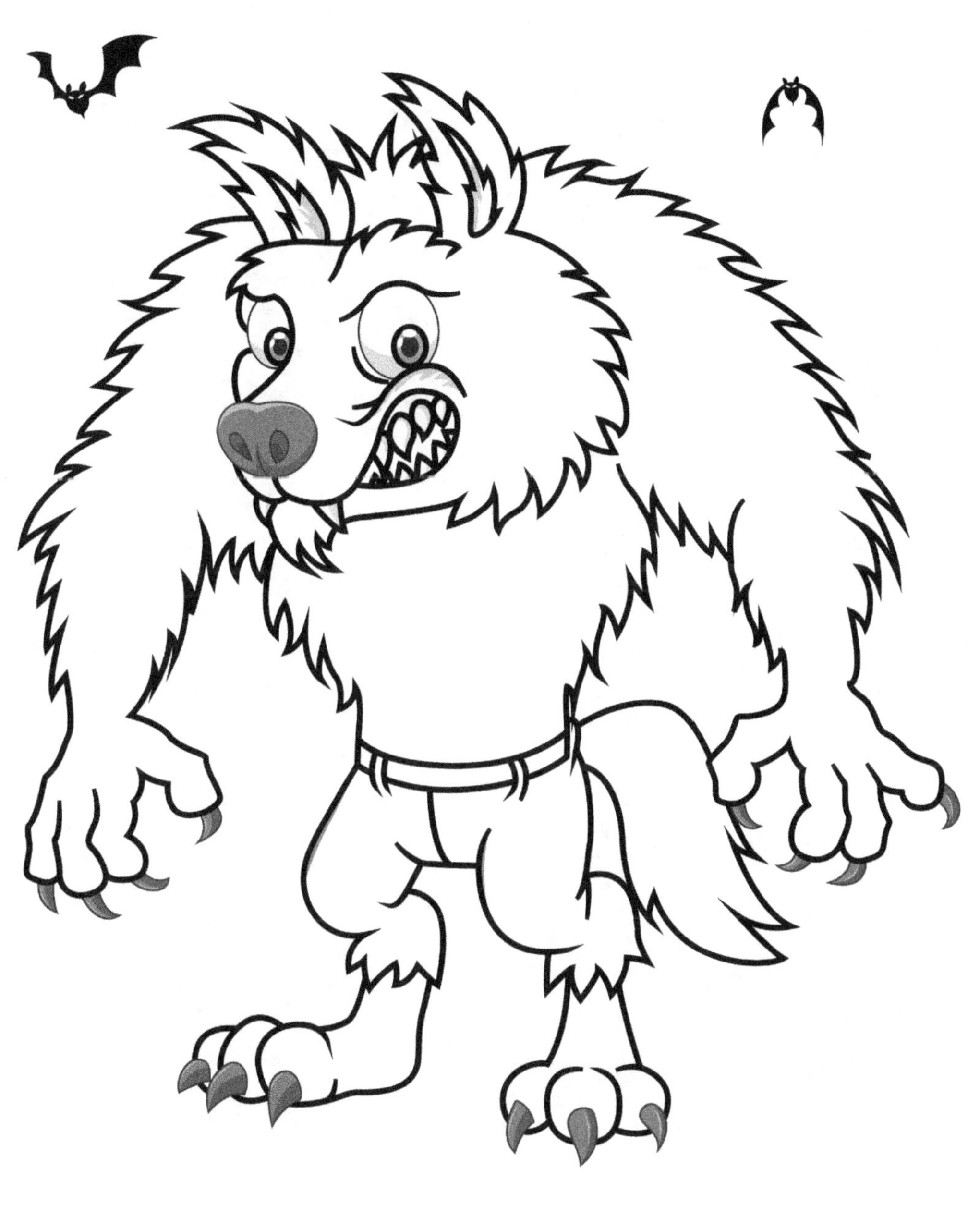

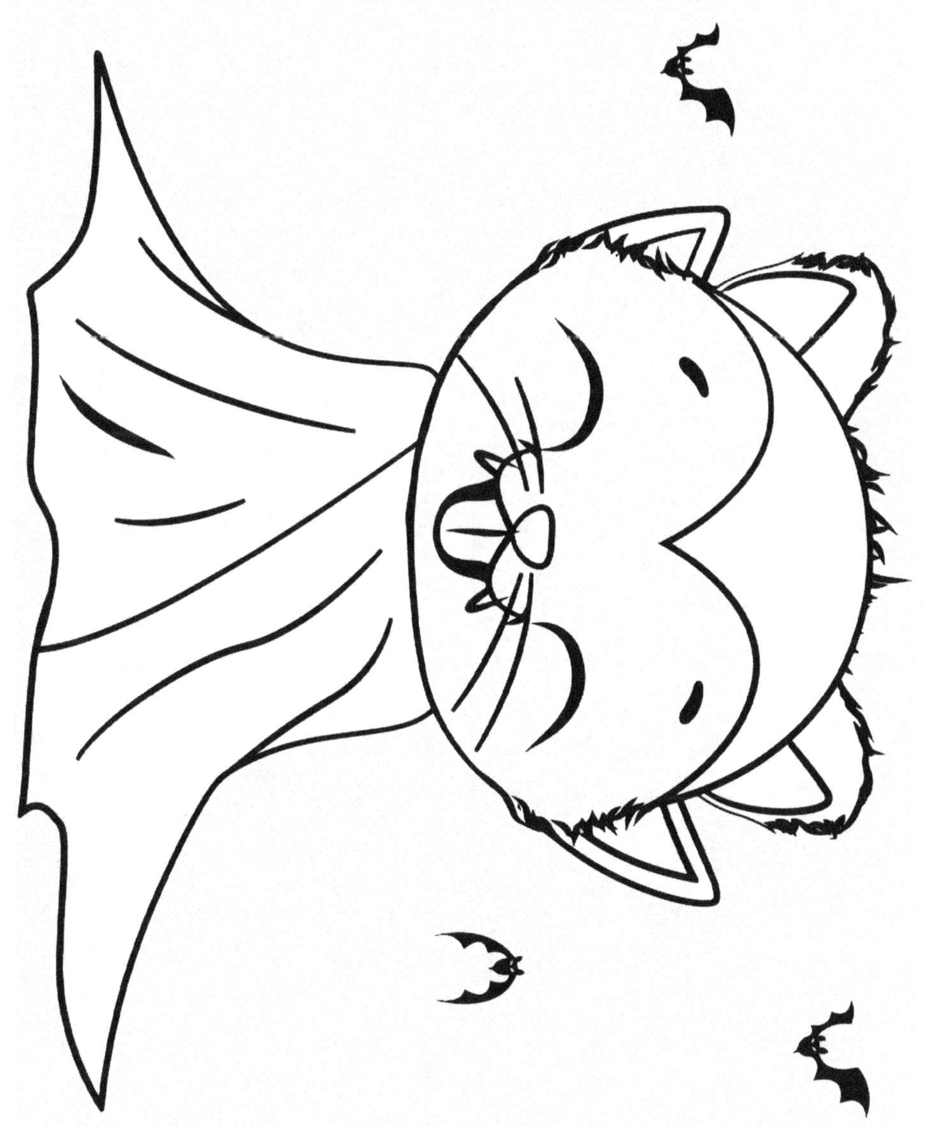

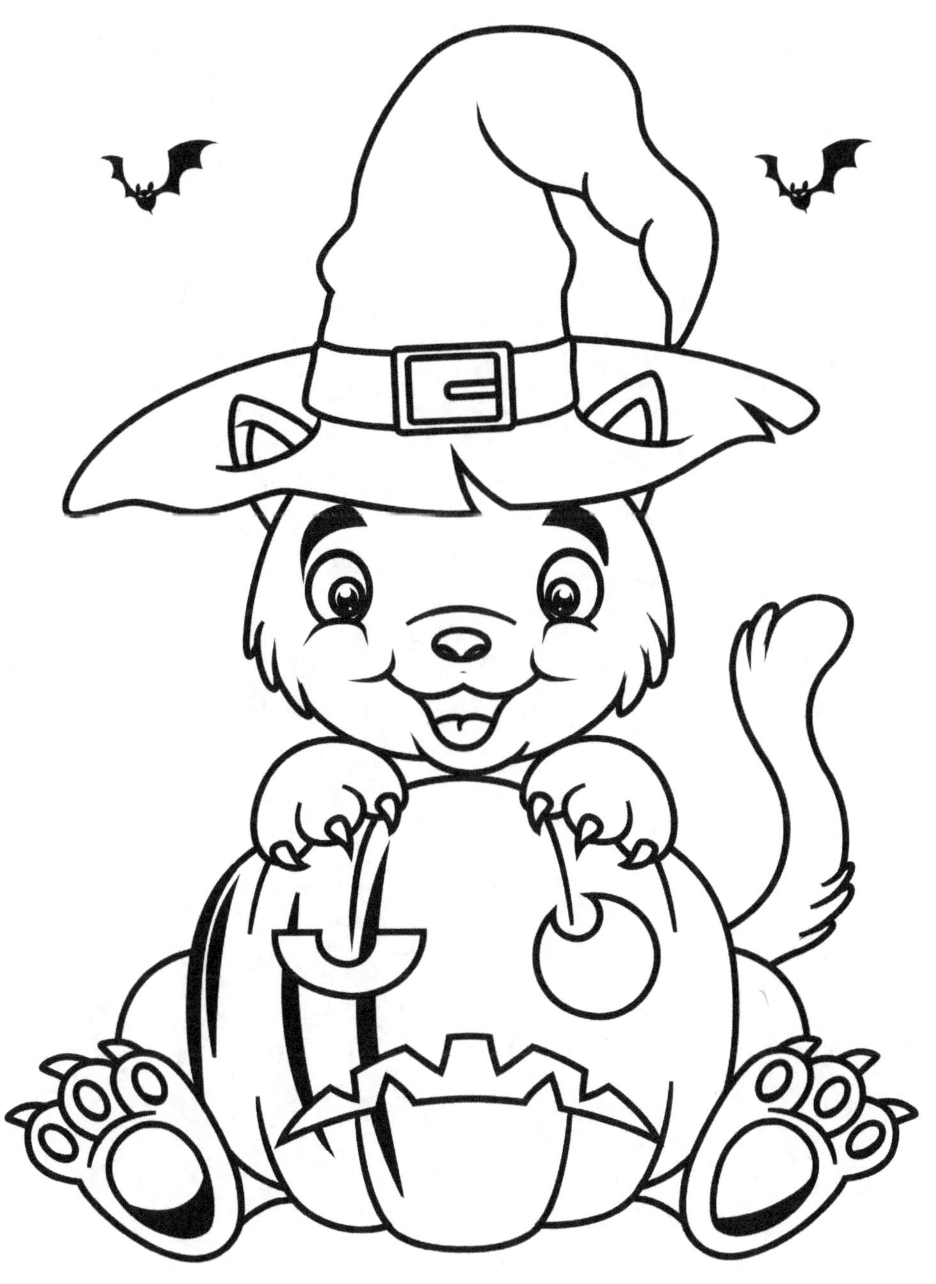

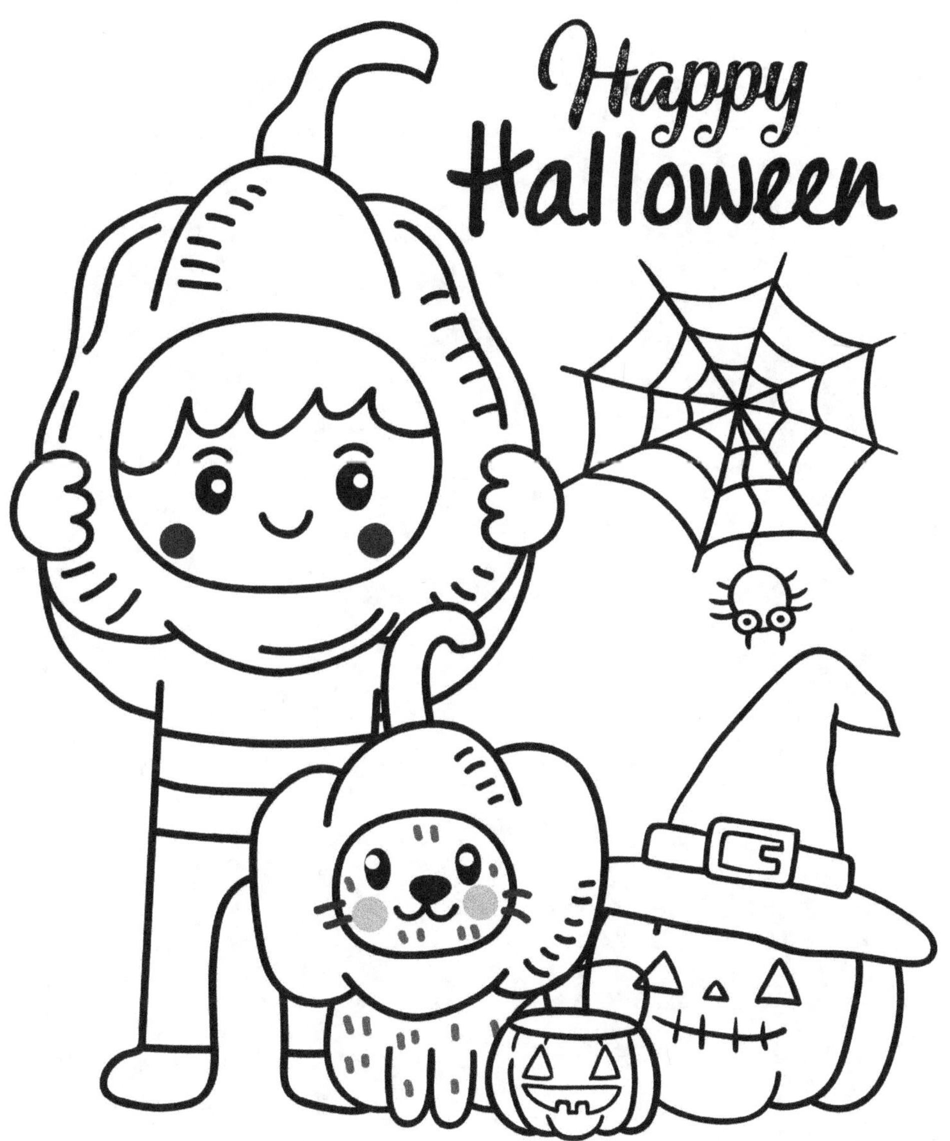
Happy
Halloween

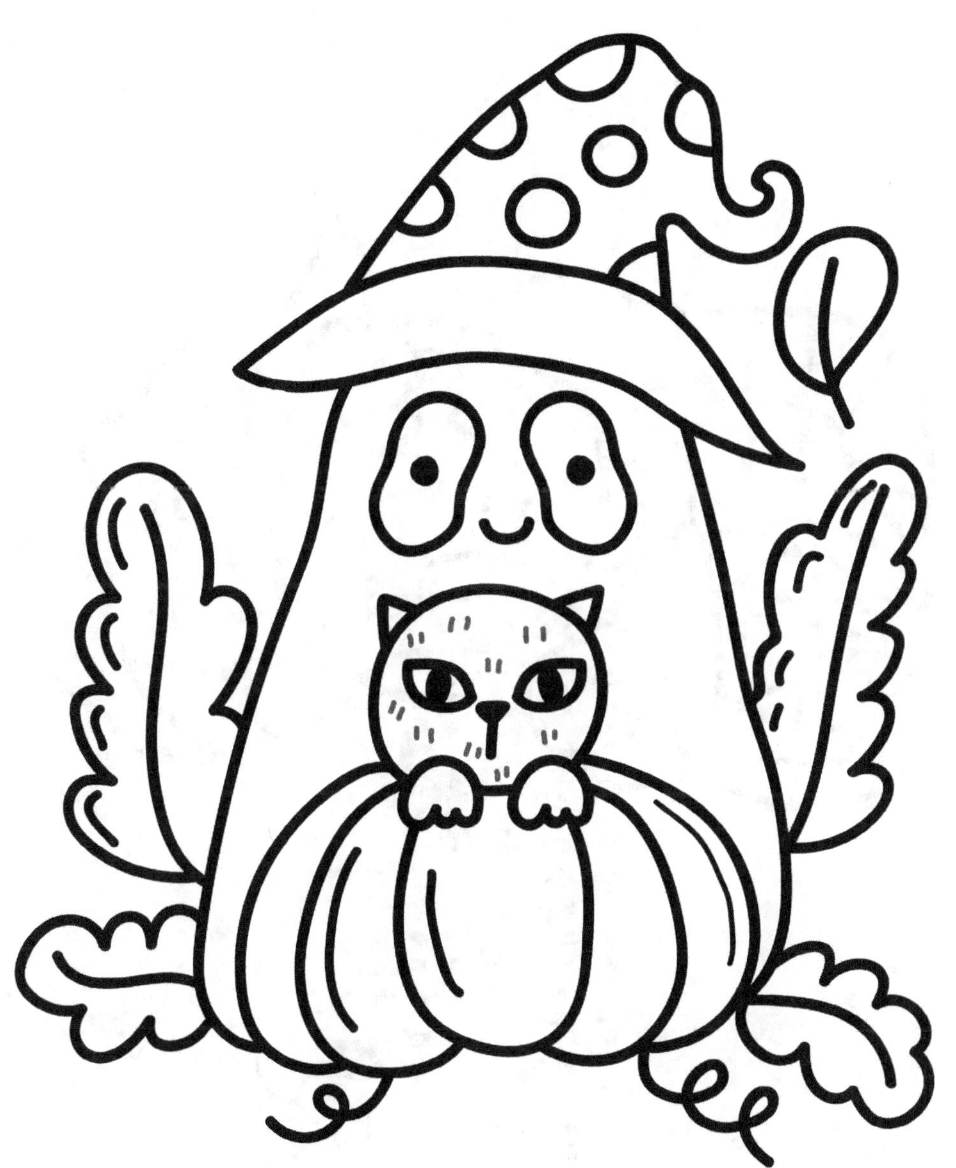

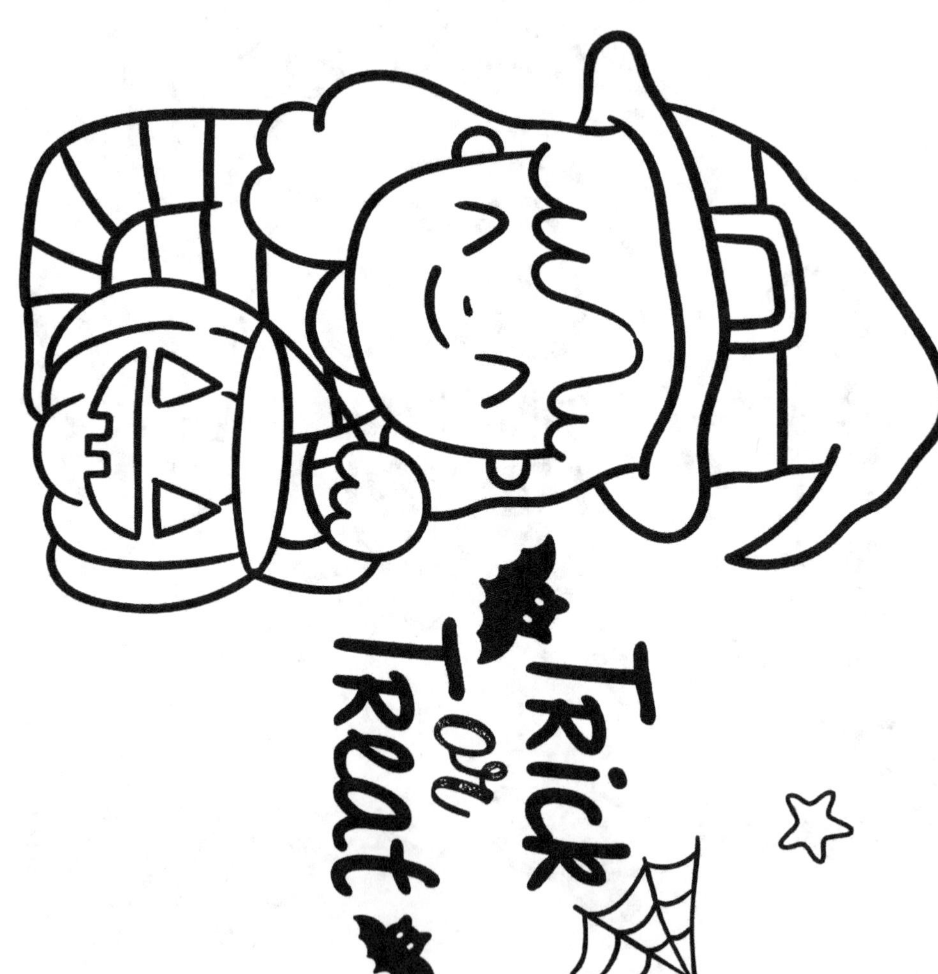

Trick
or
Treat

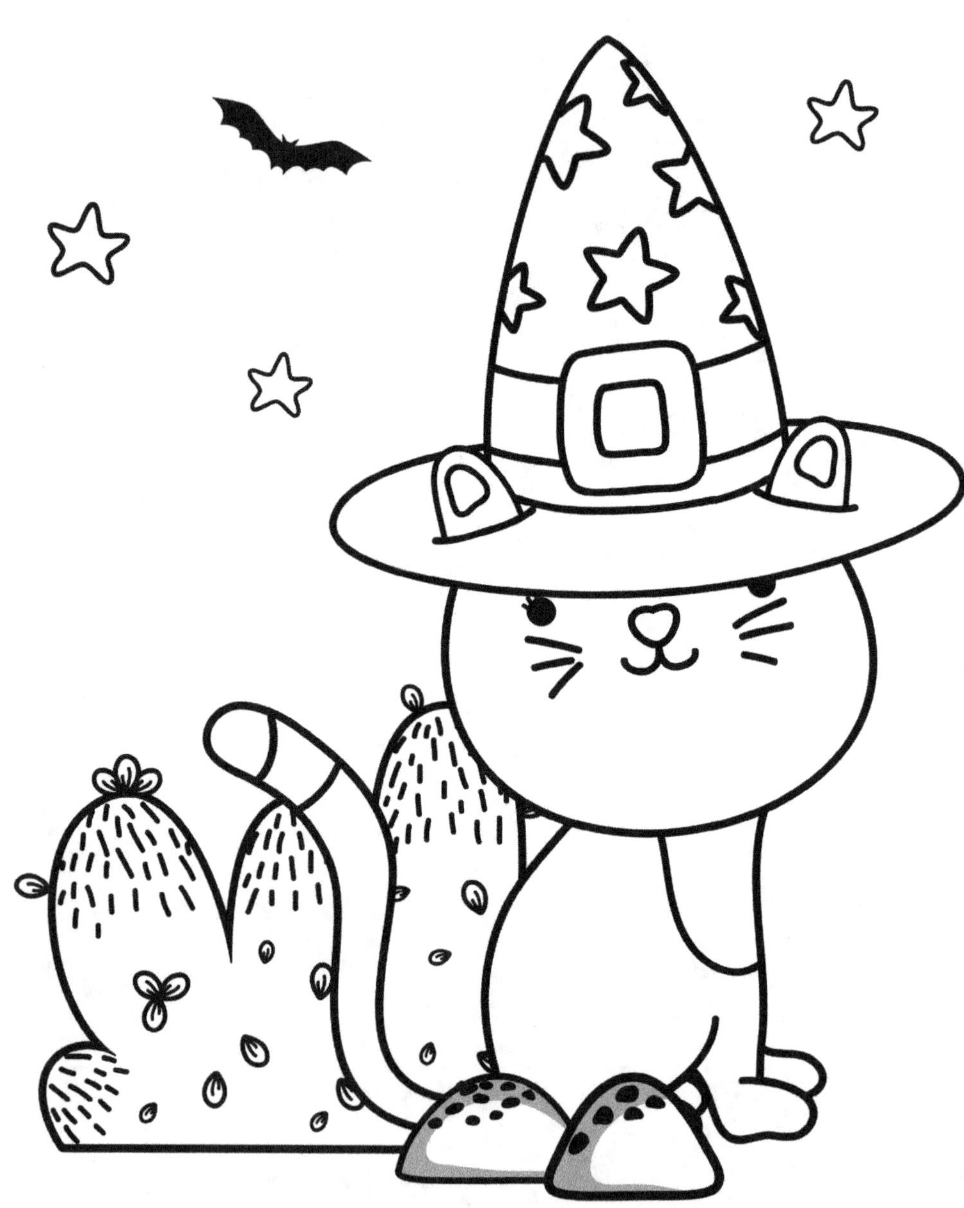

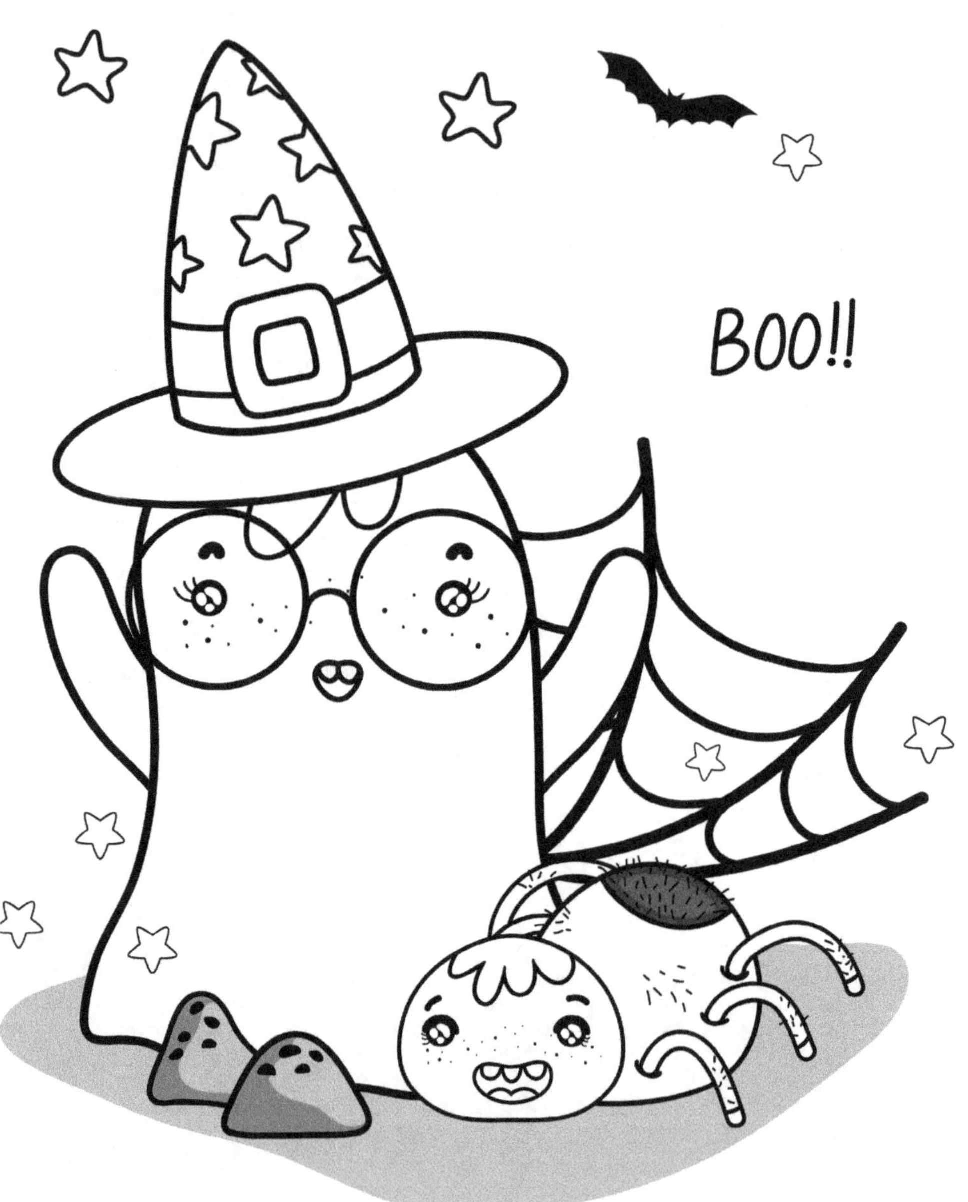
BOO!!

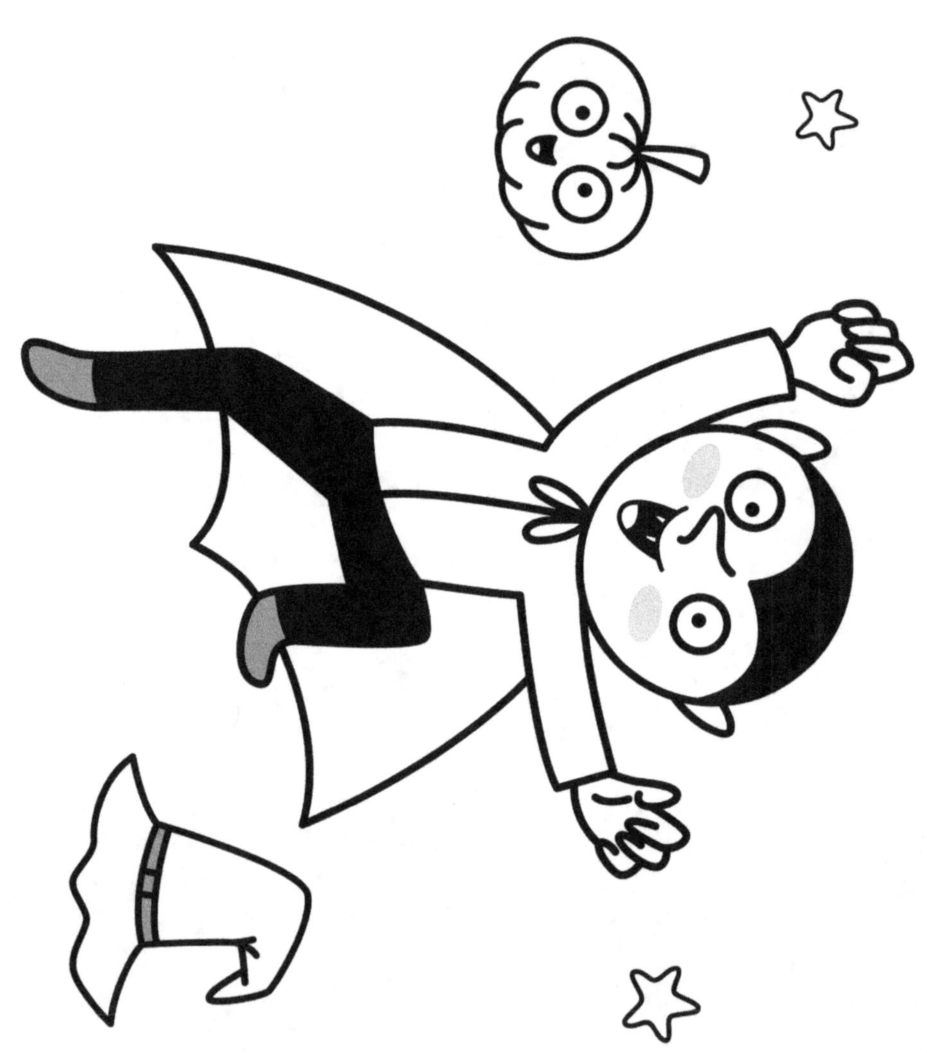

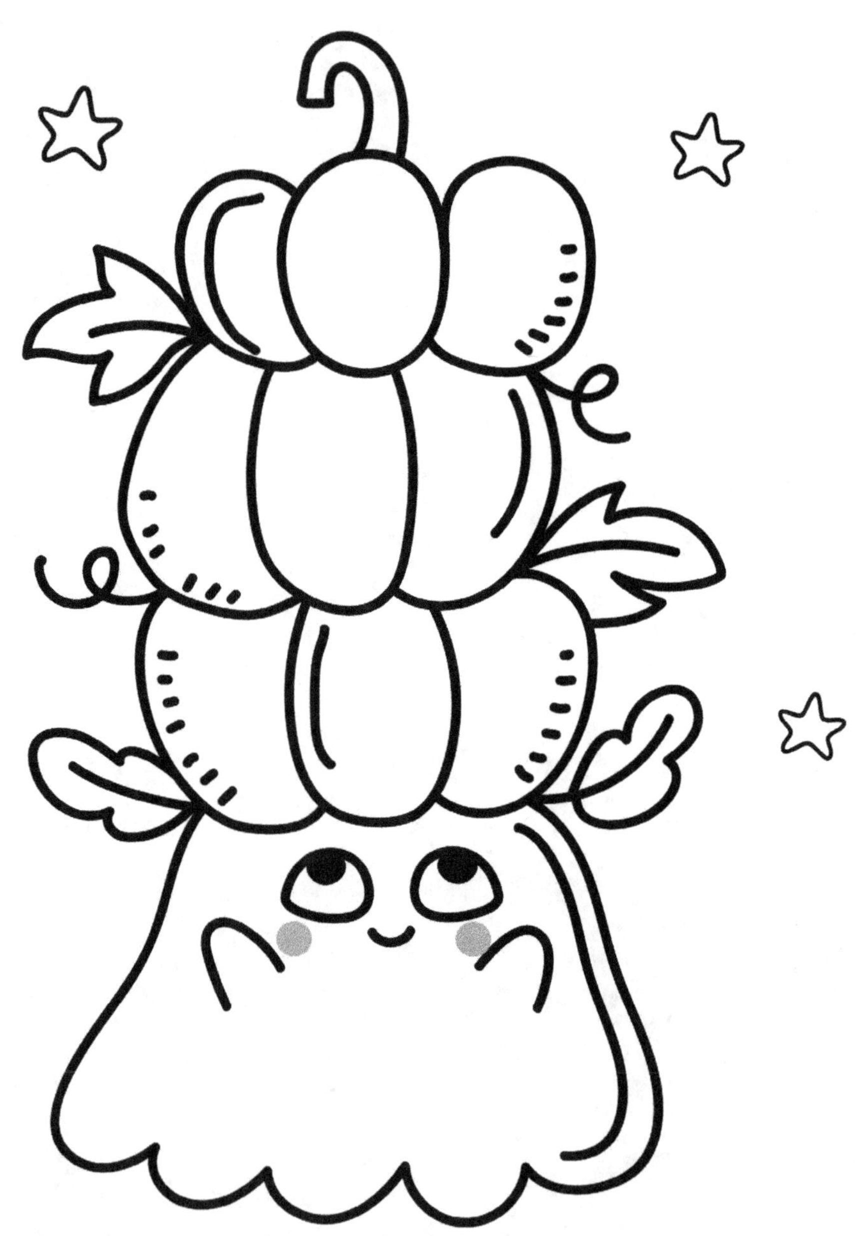

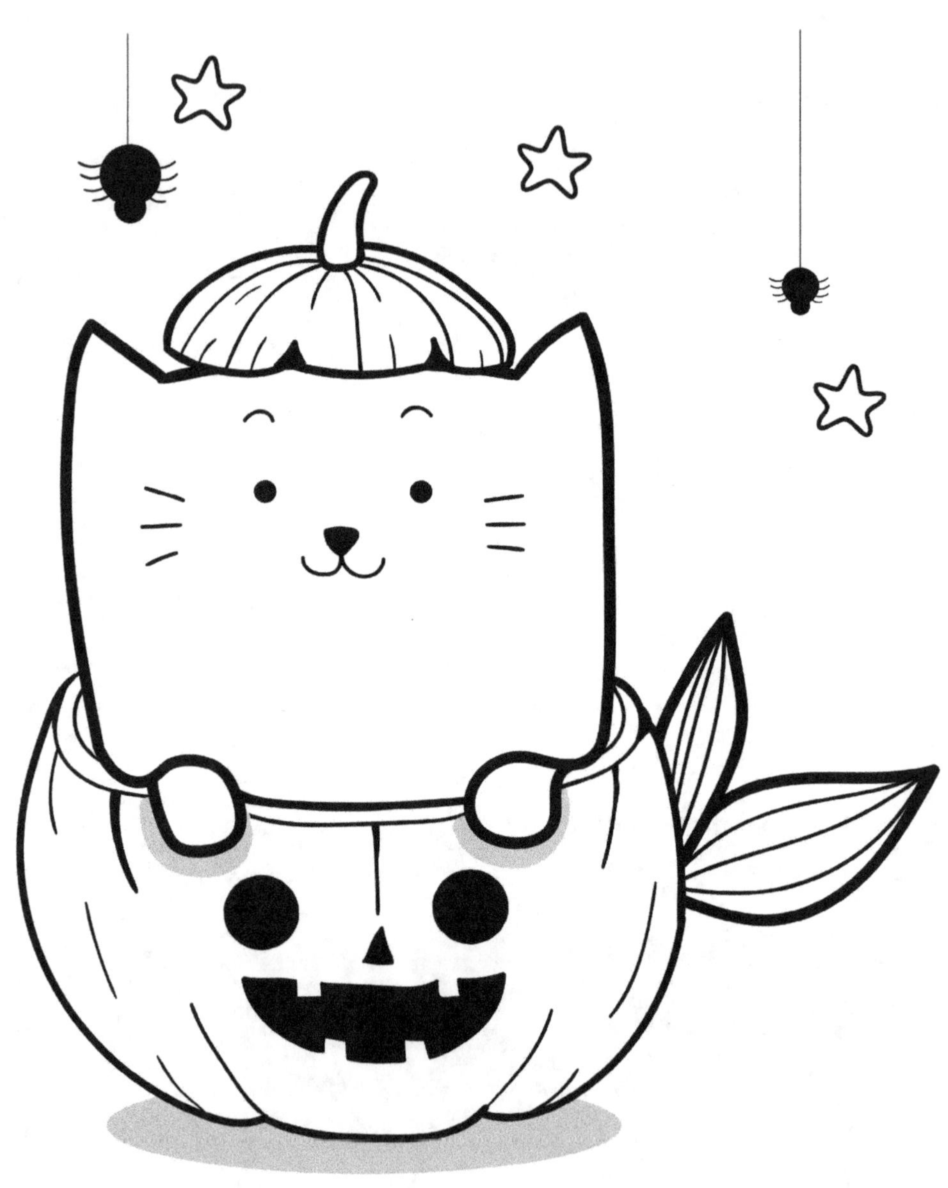

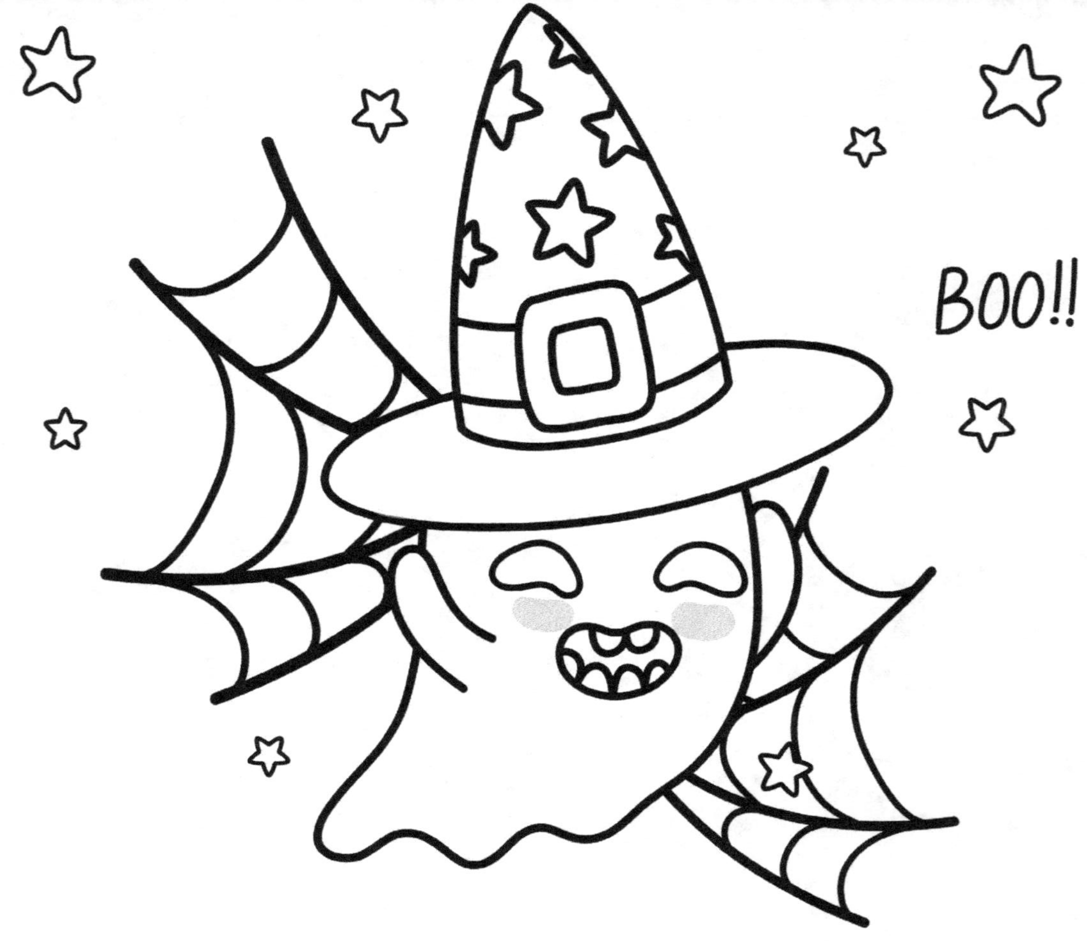

BOO!!

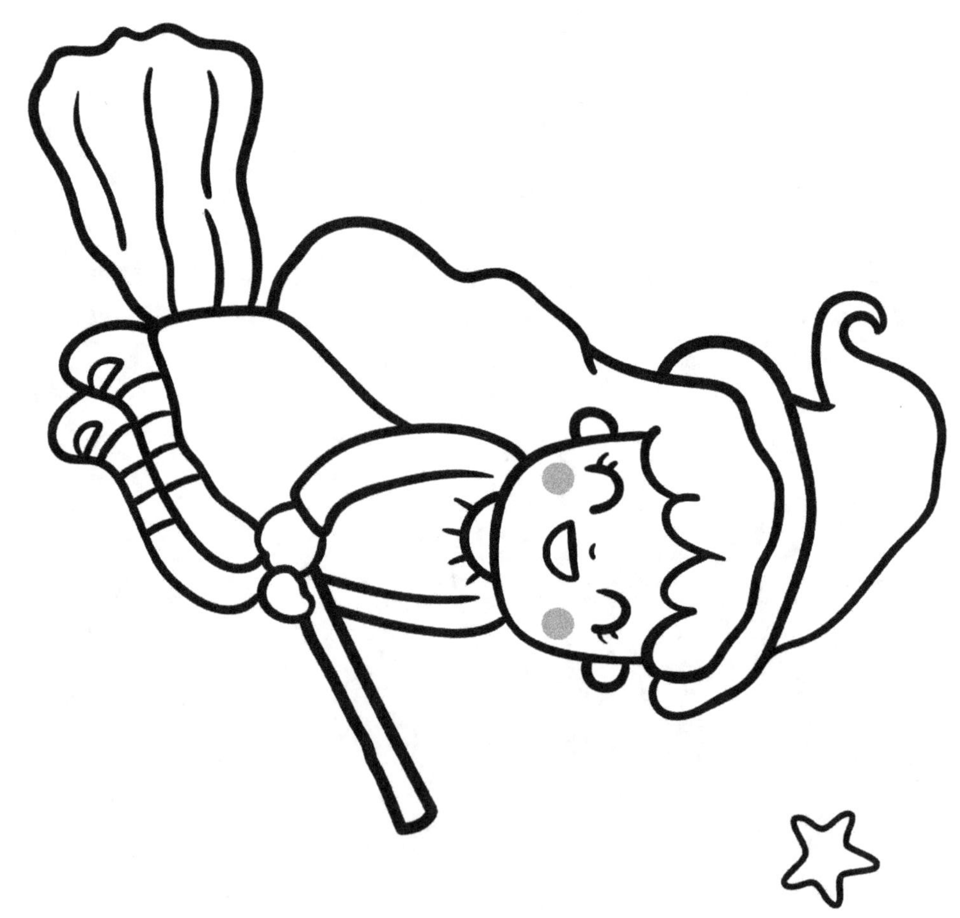

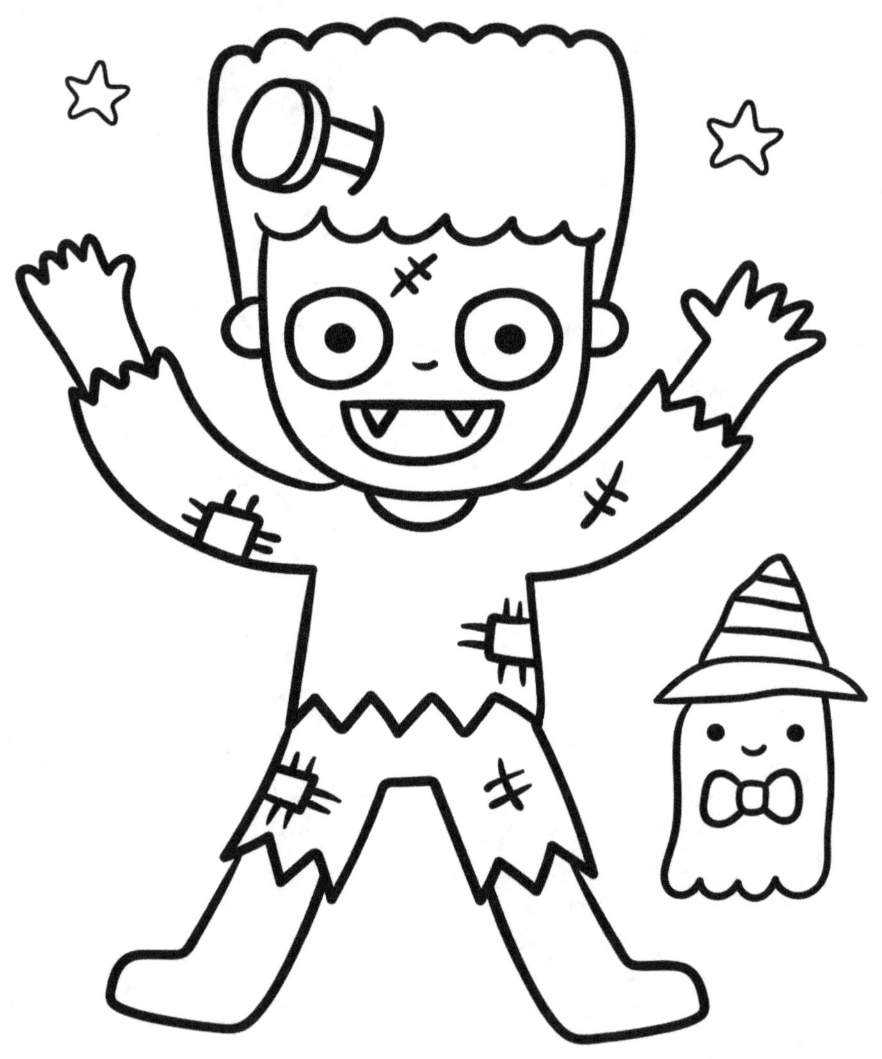

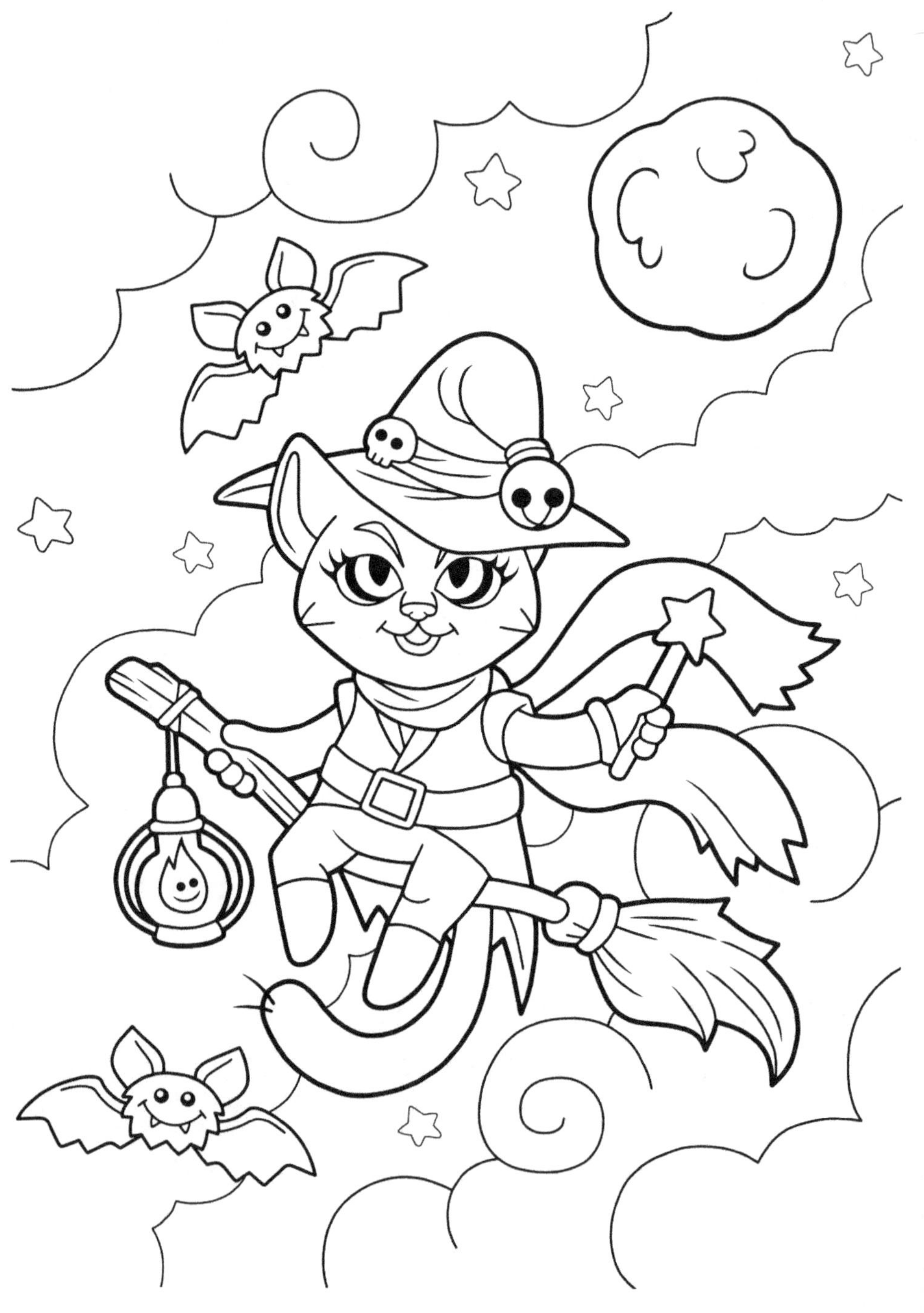

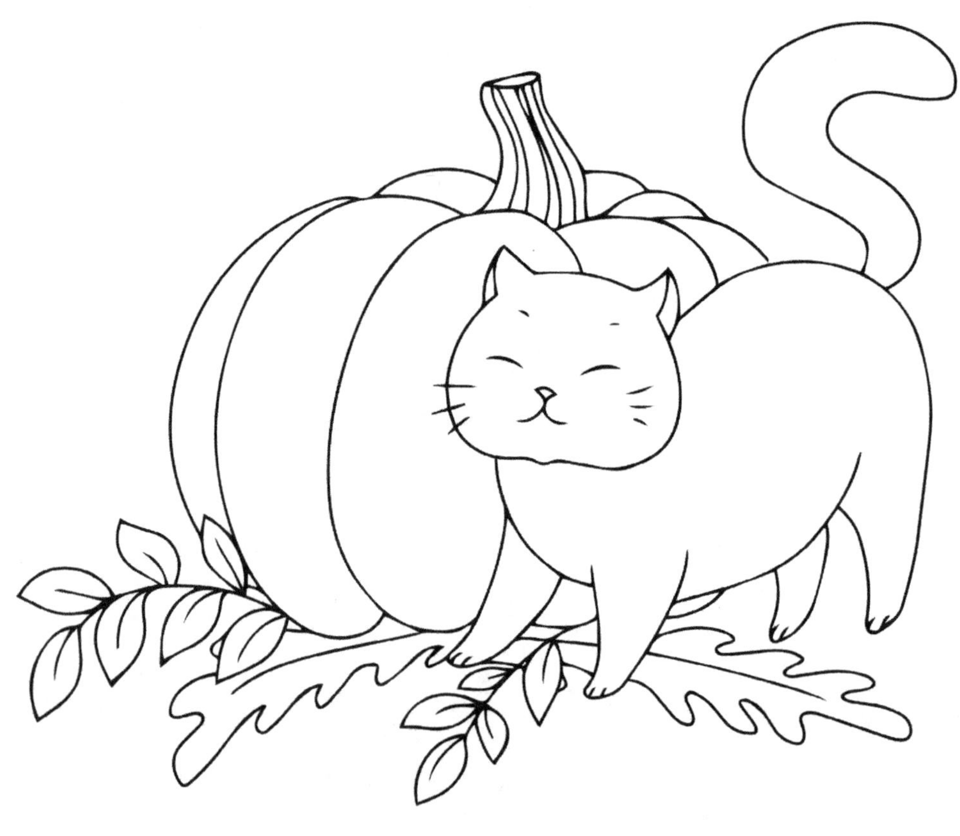

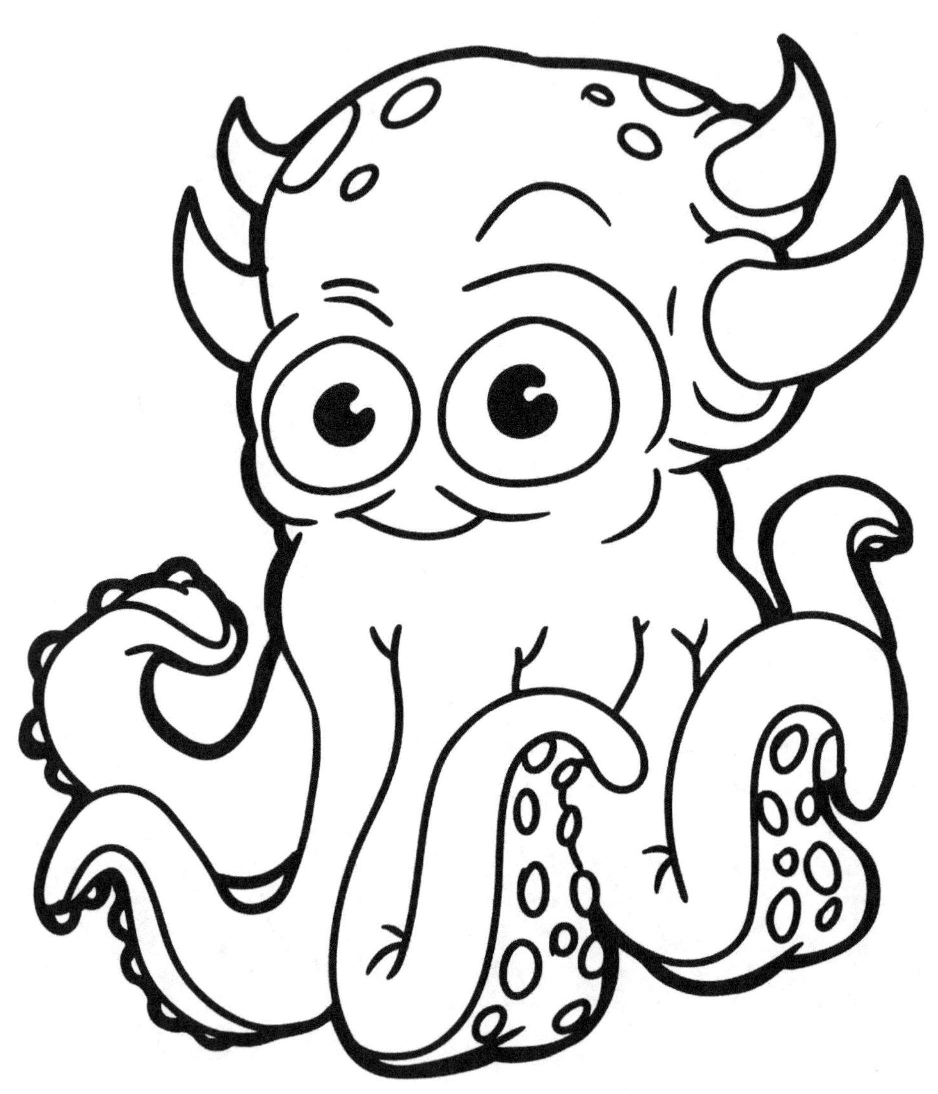

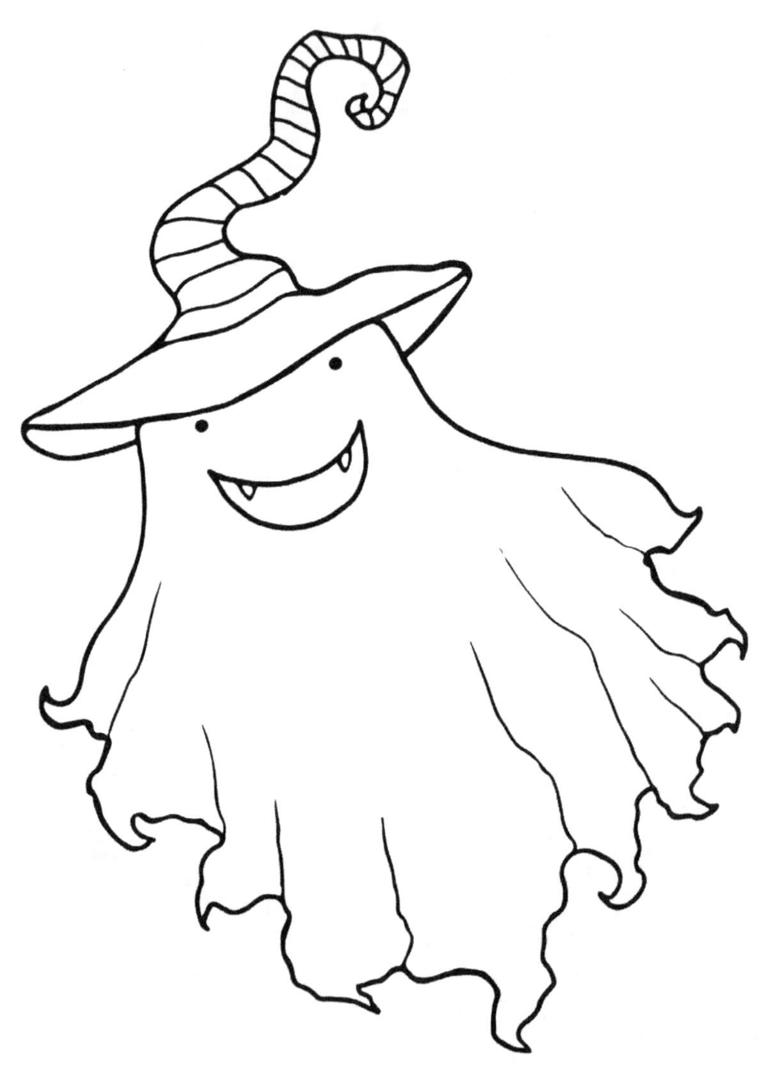

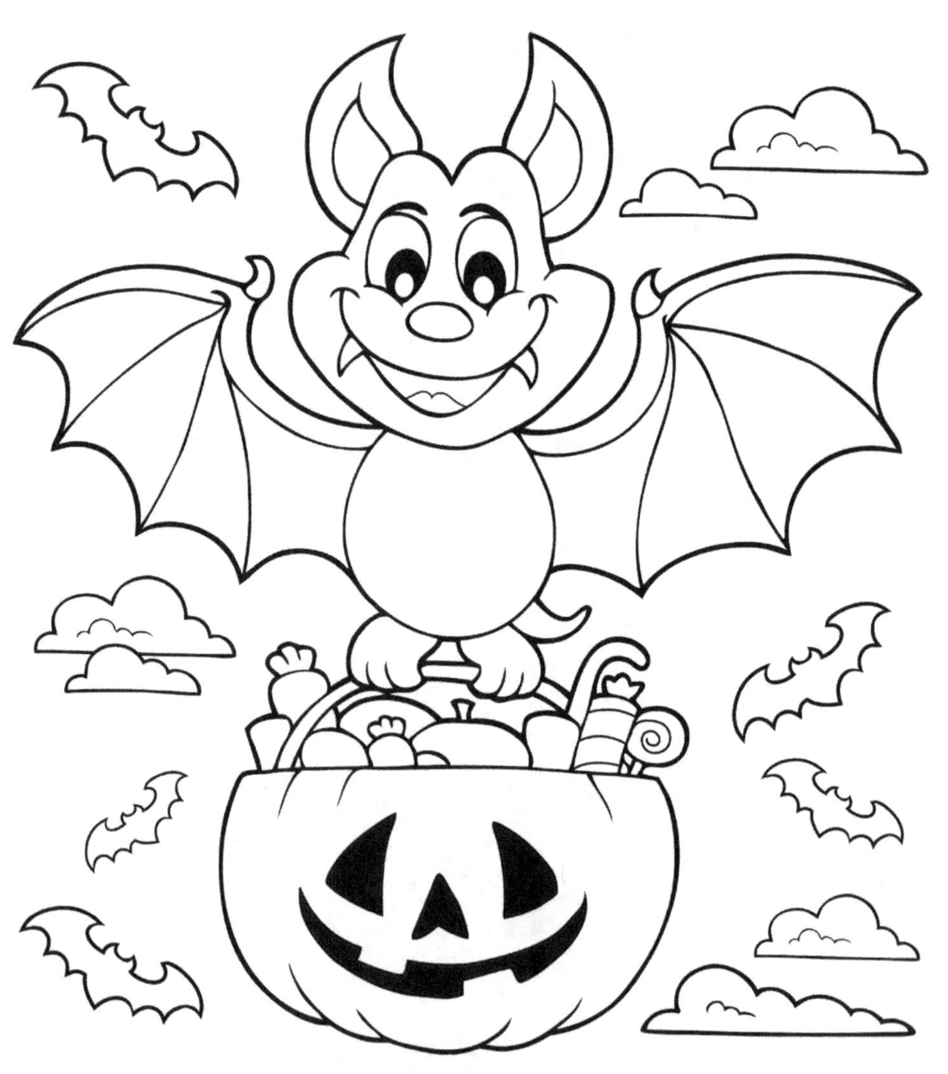

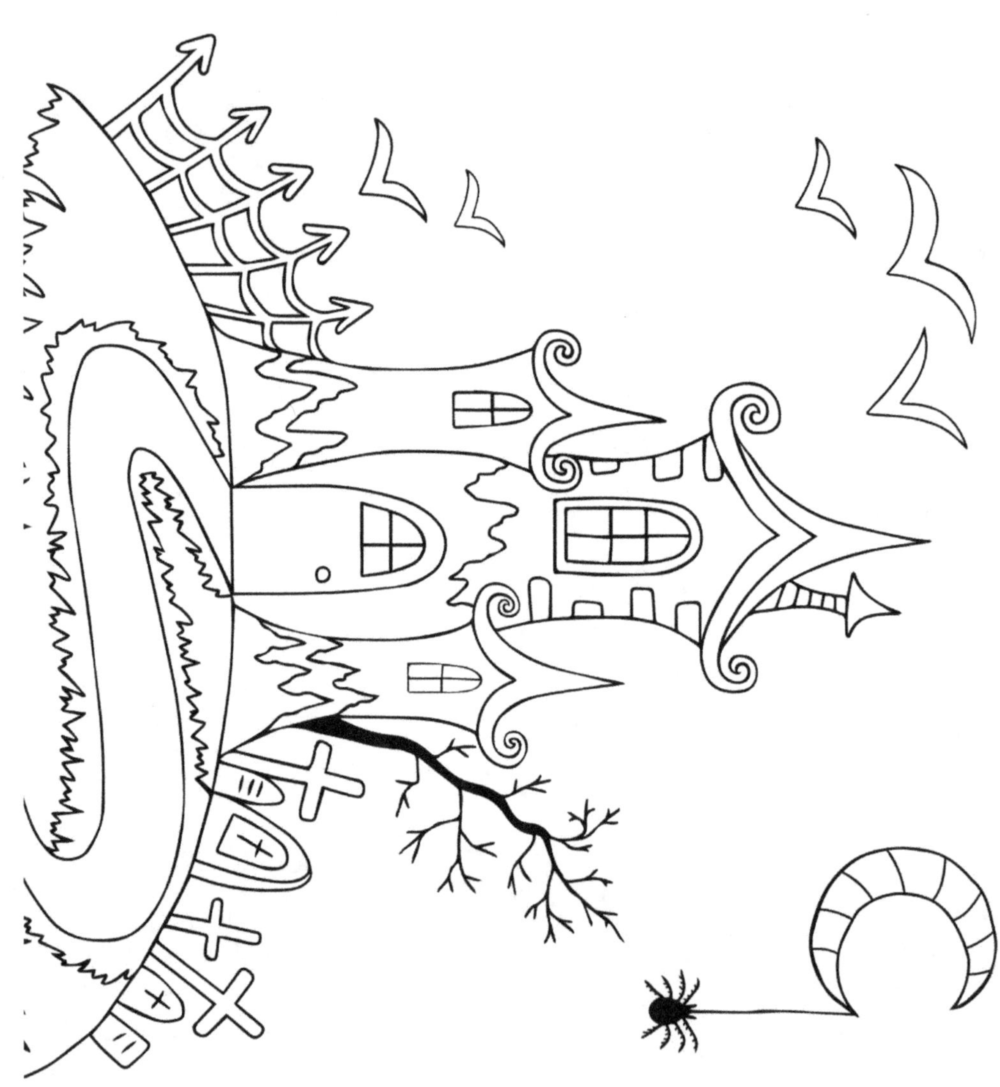

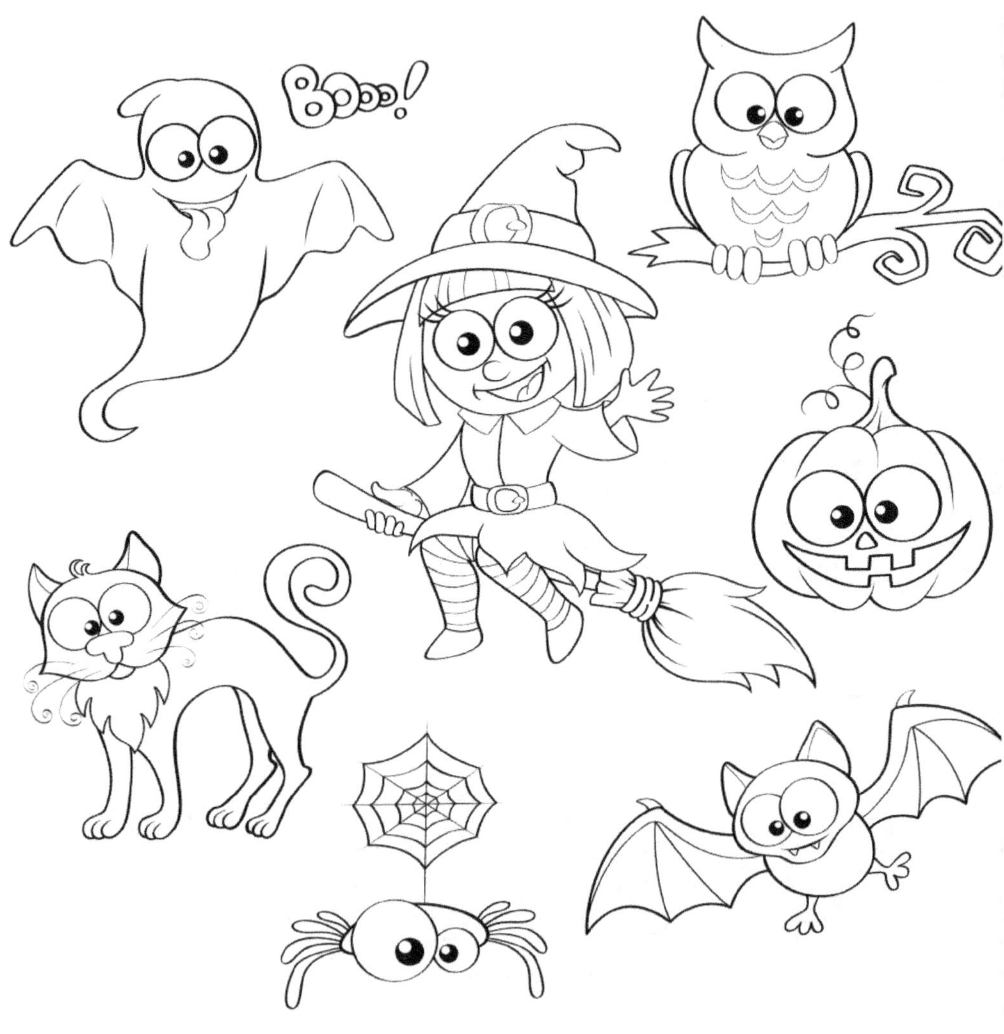

Booo!

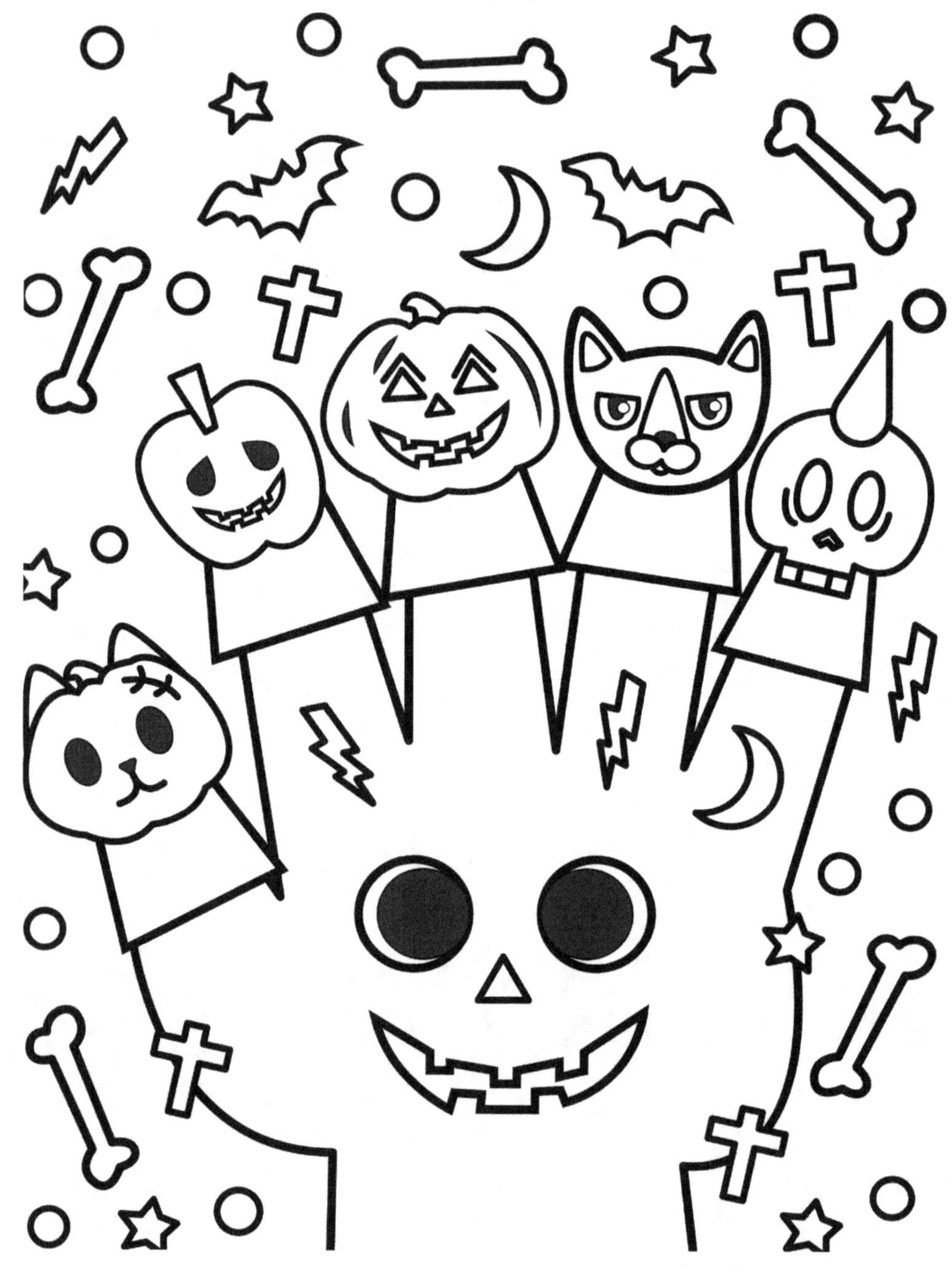

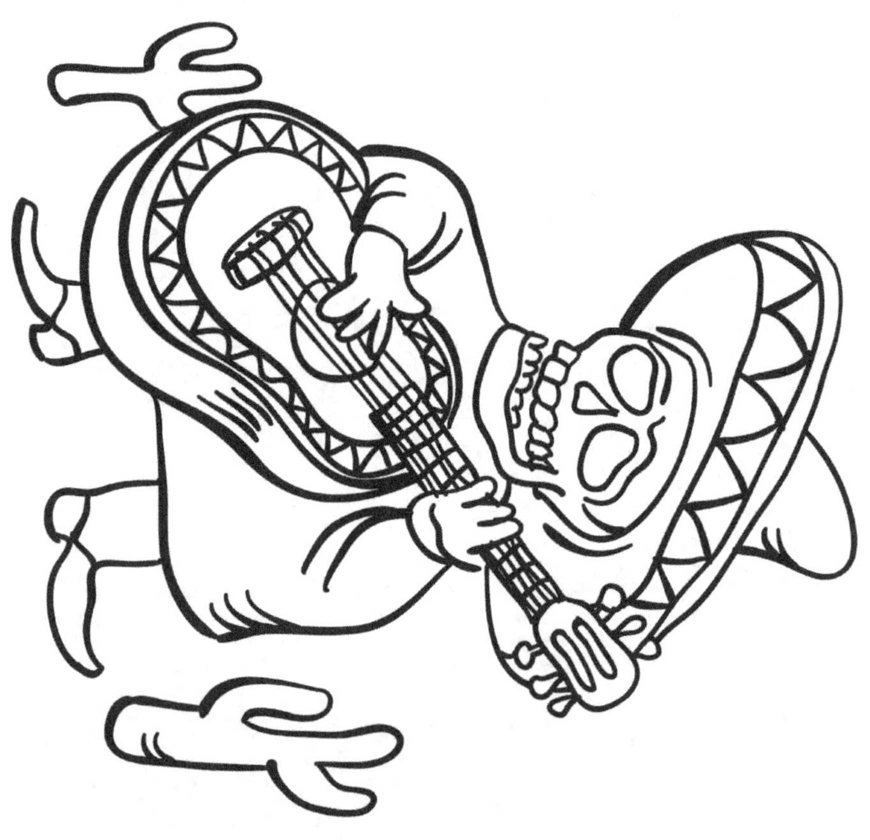

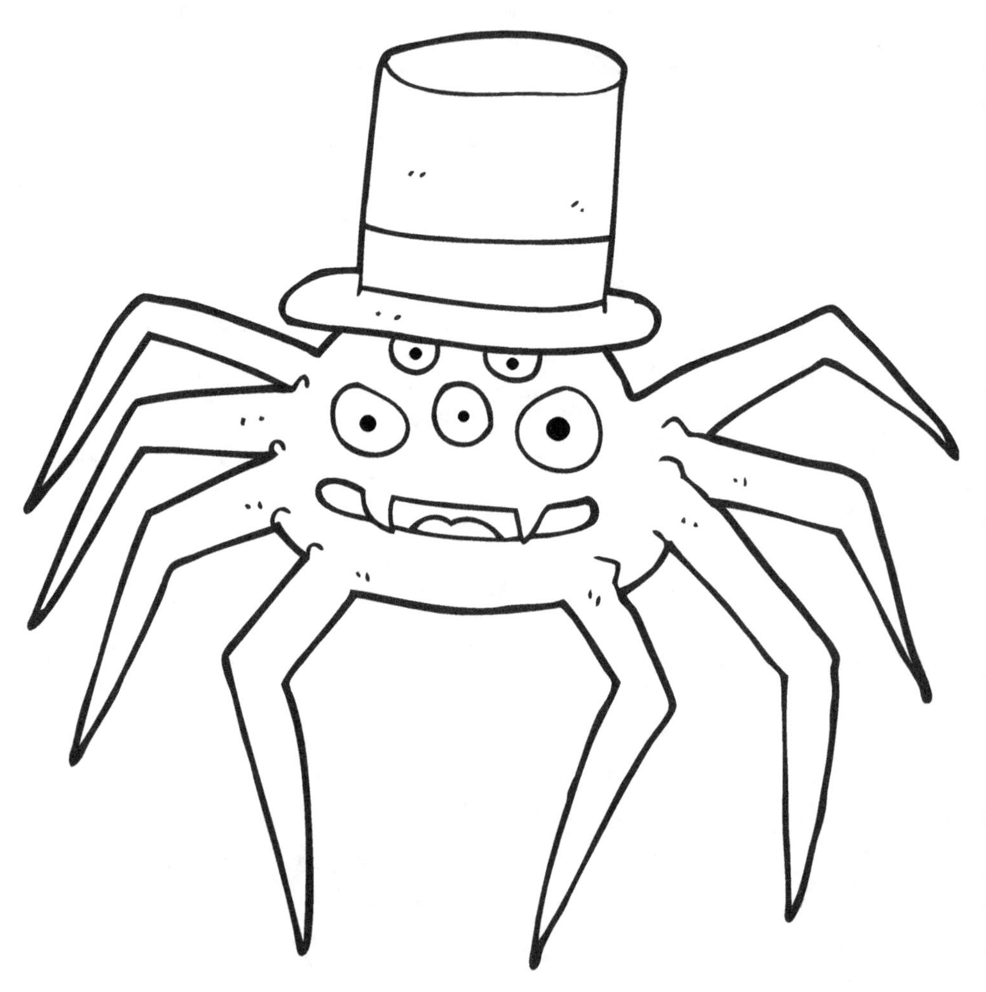

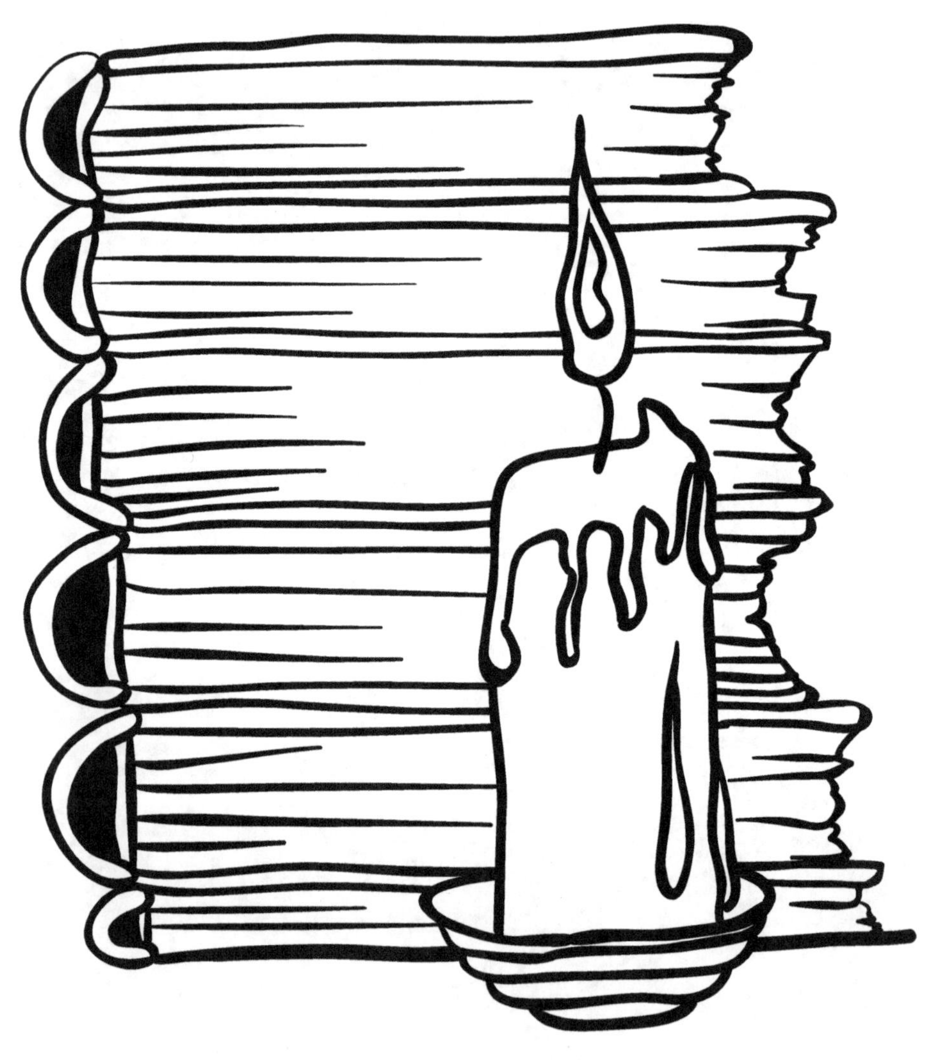

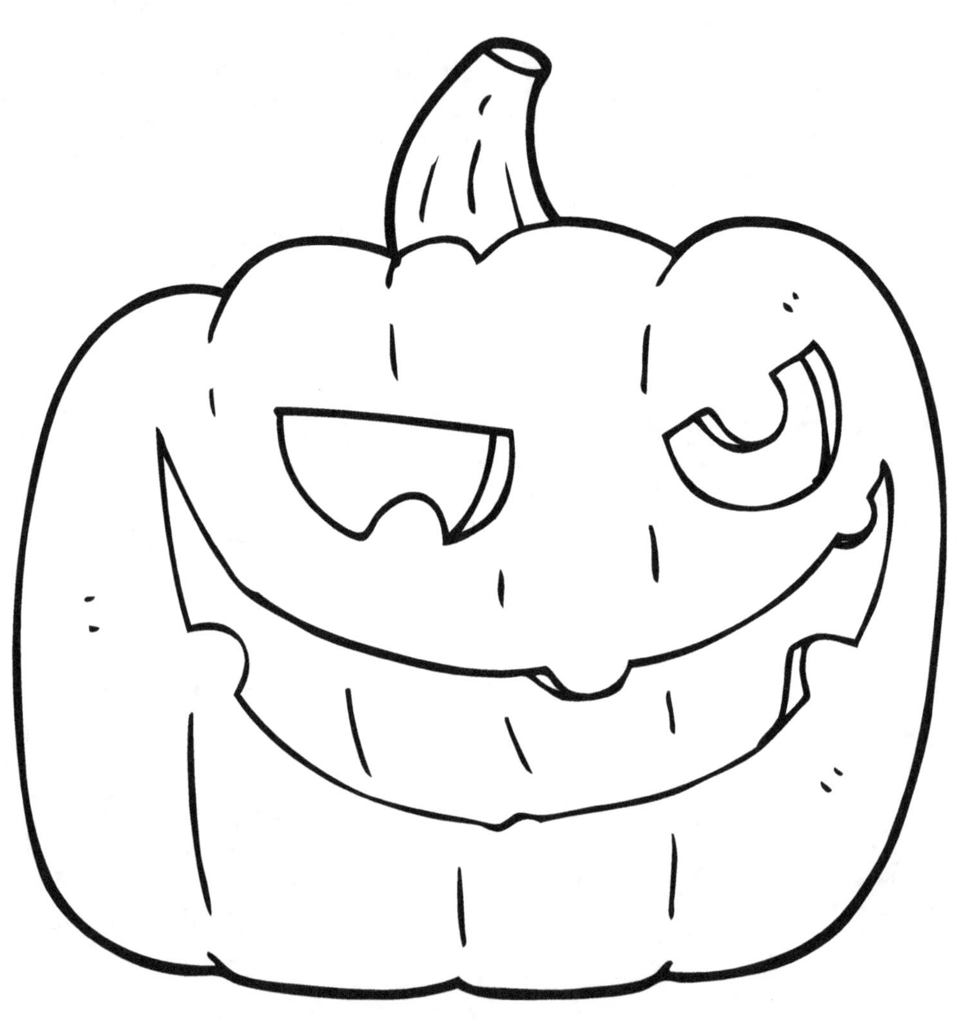

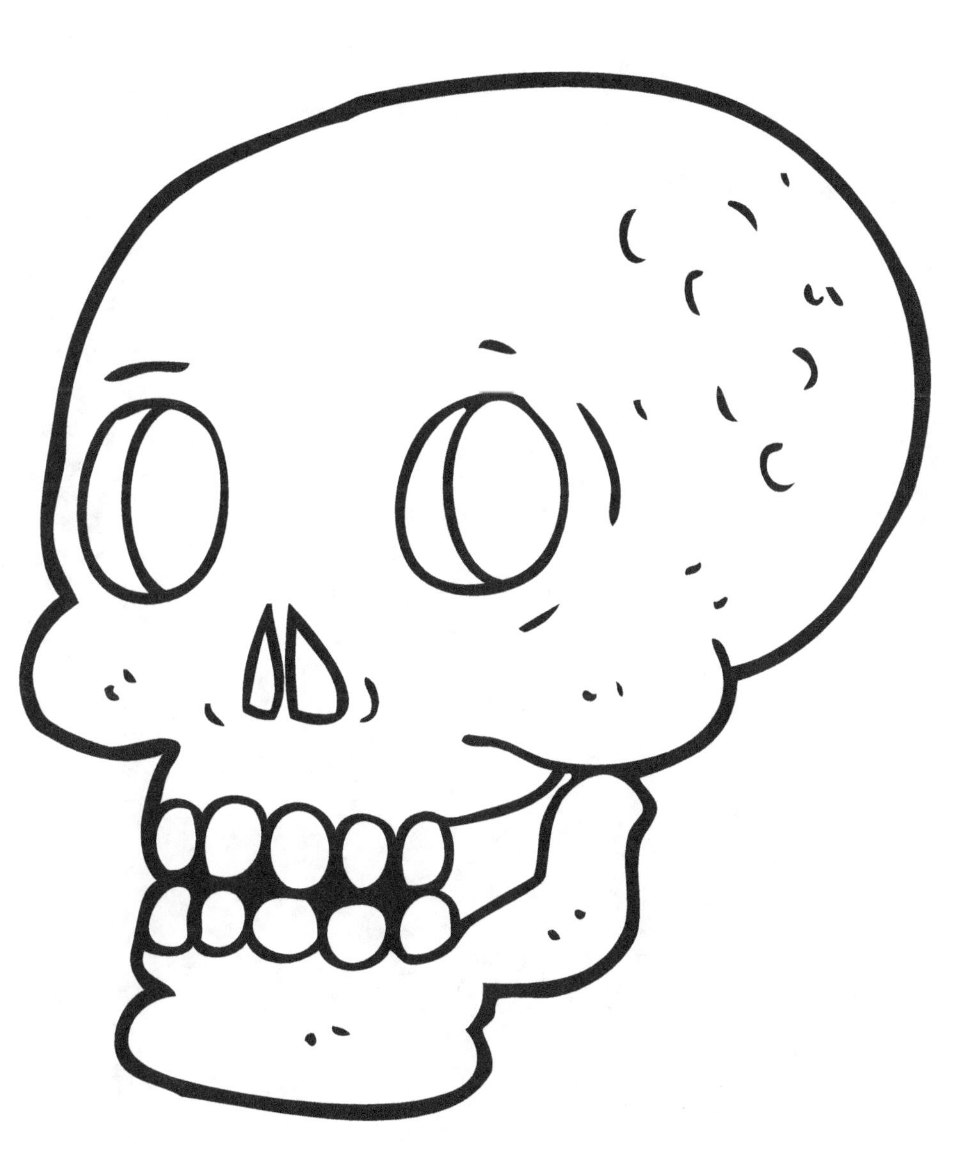

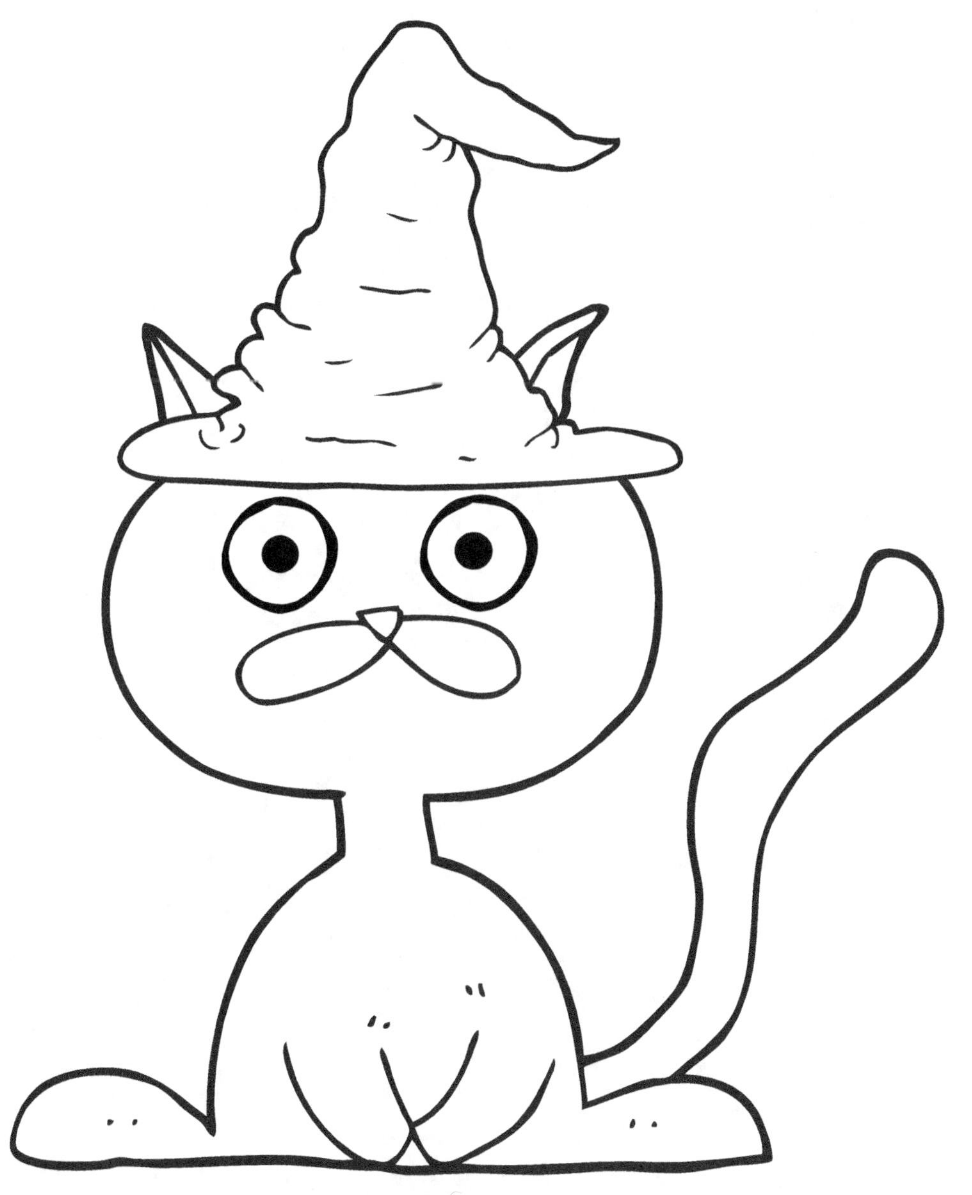

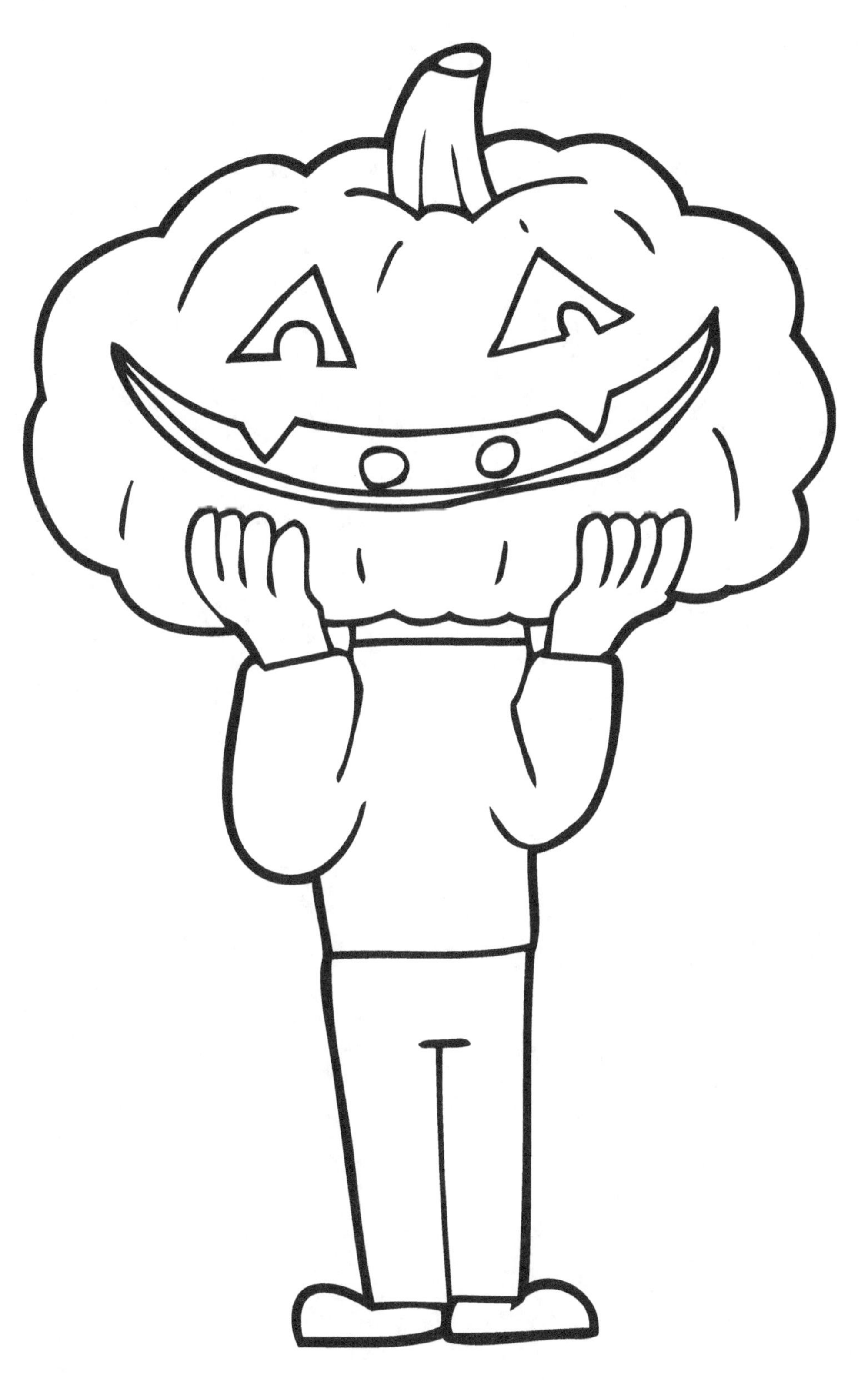

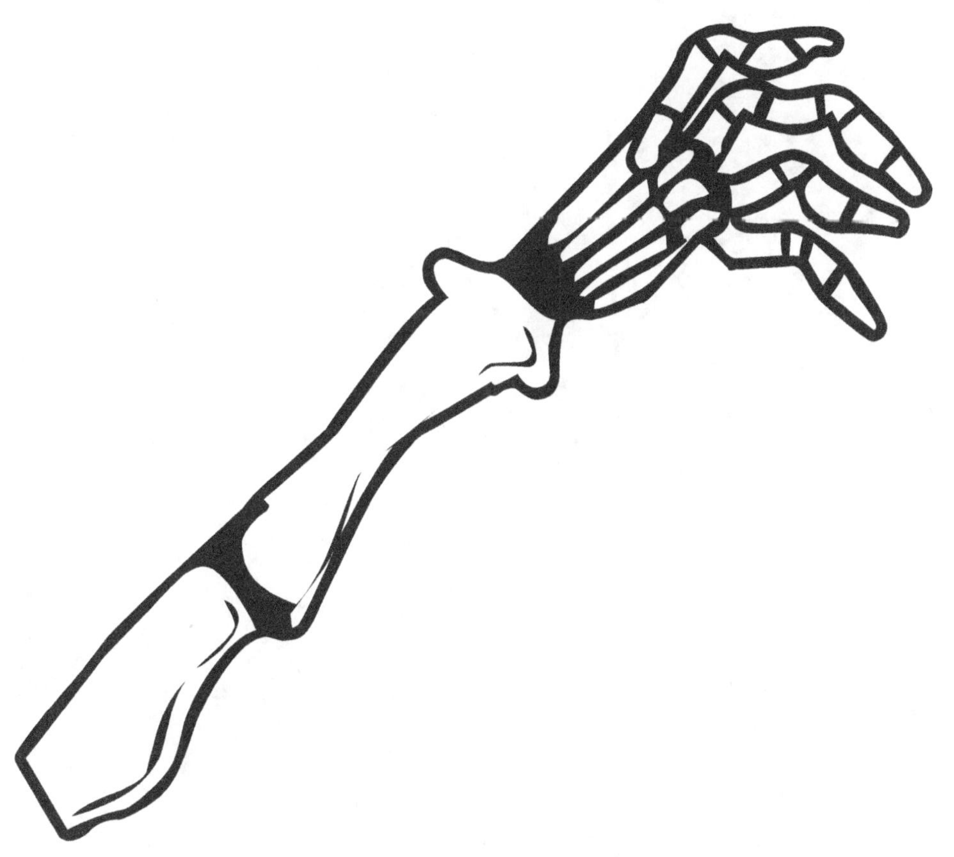

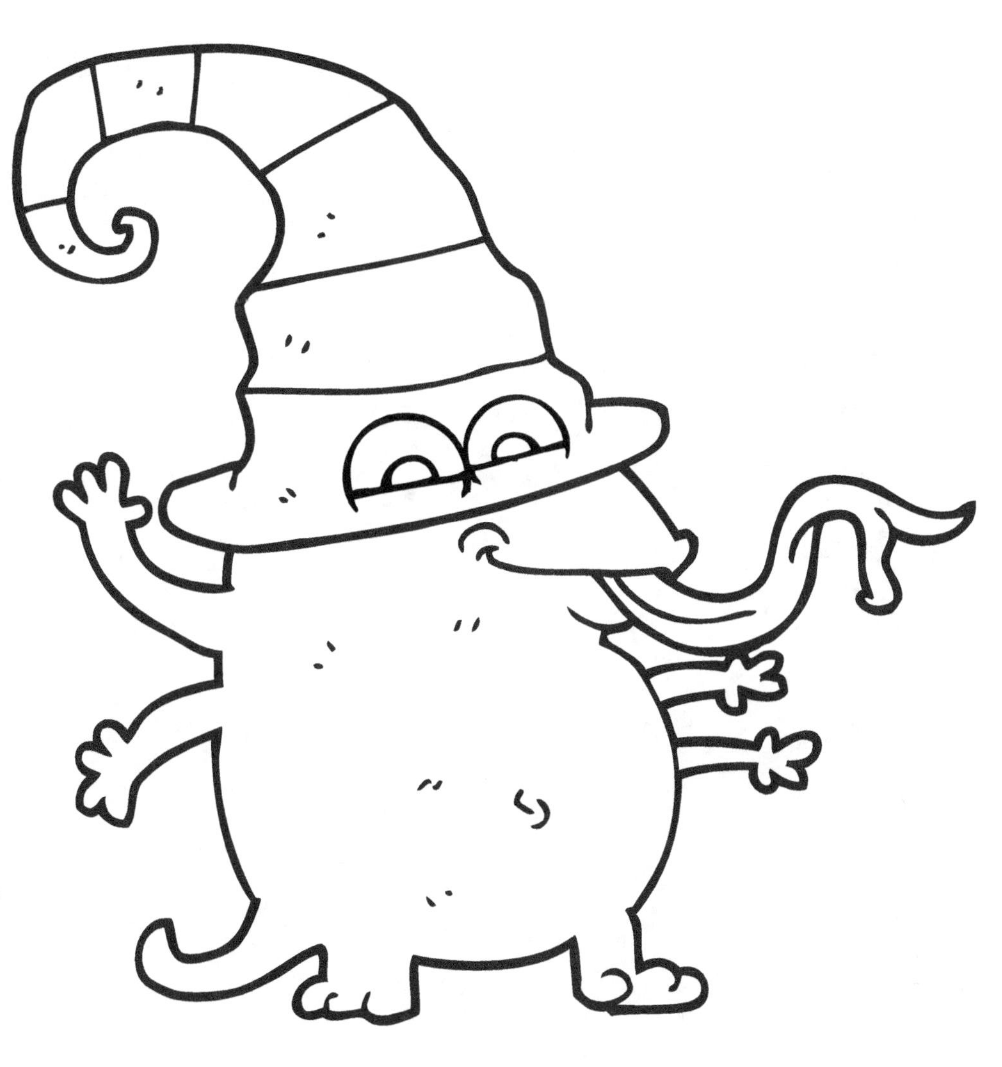

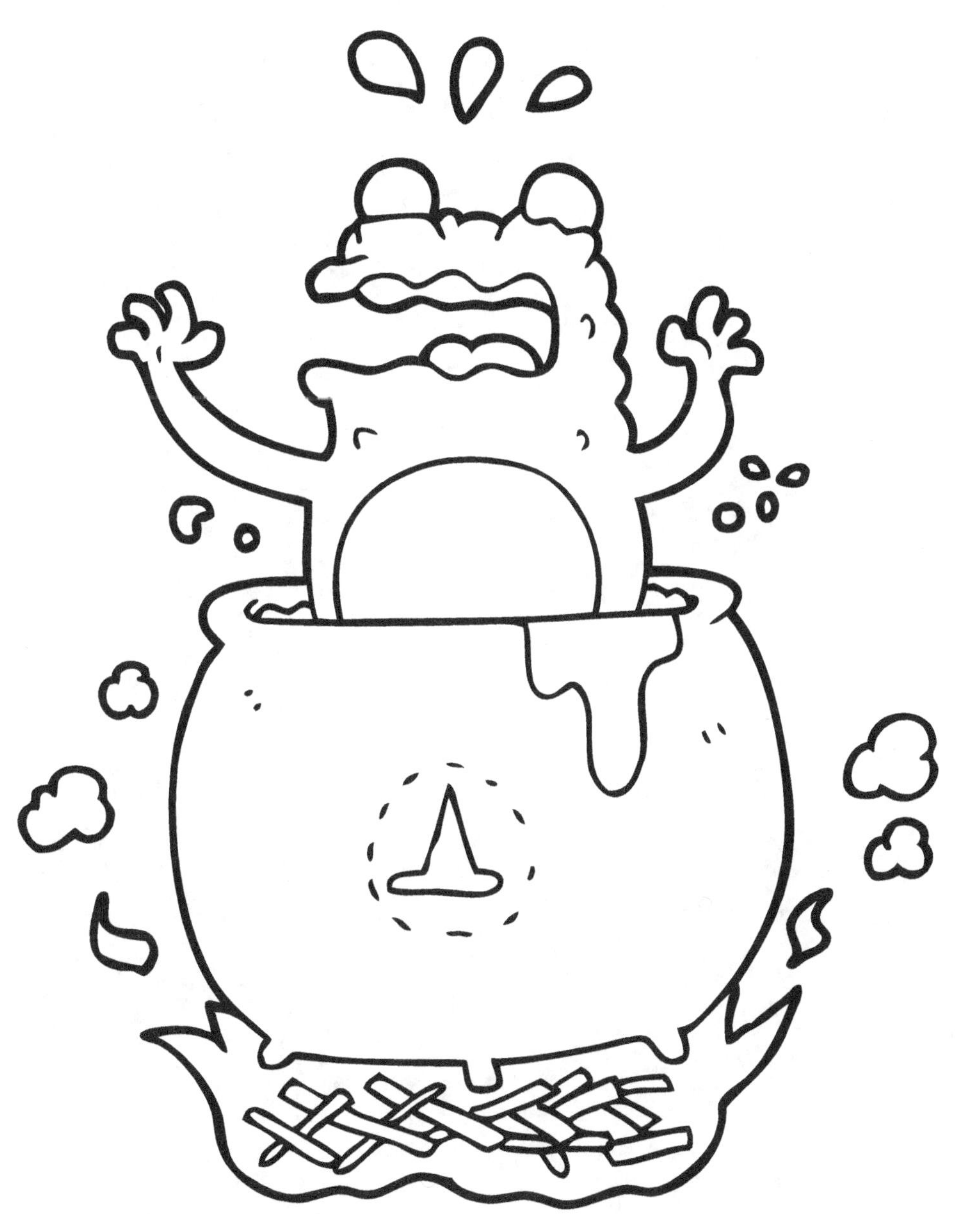

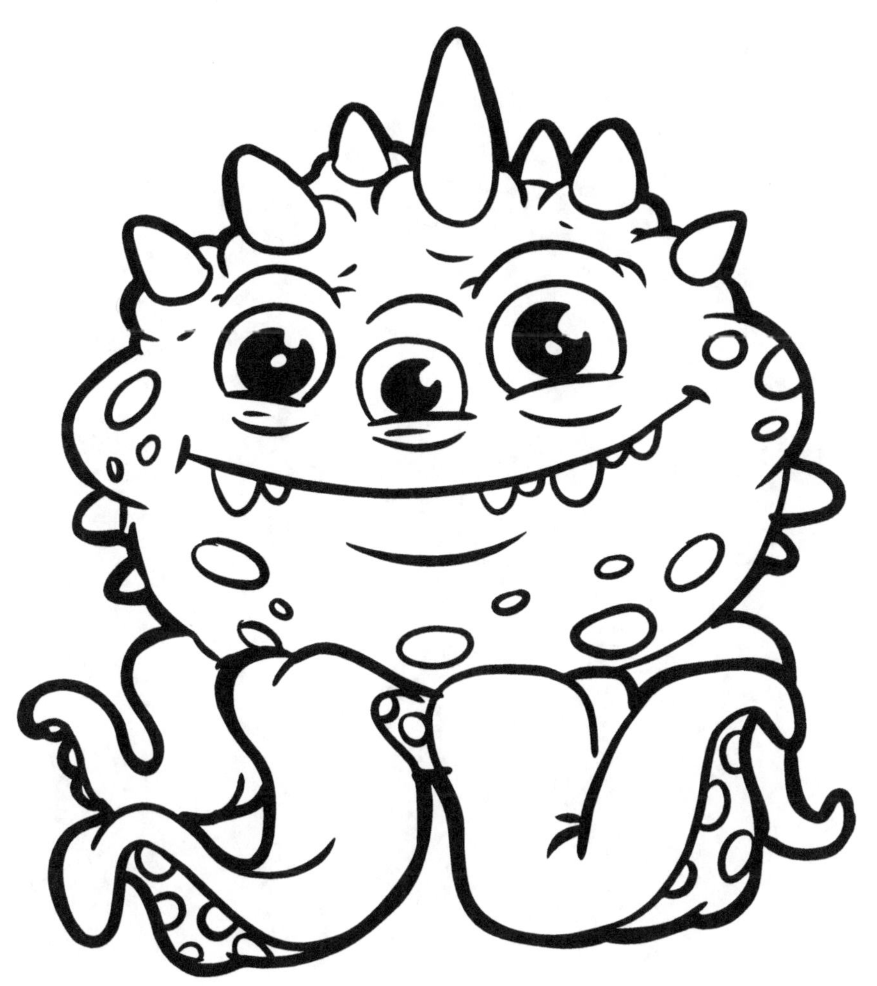

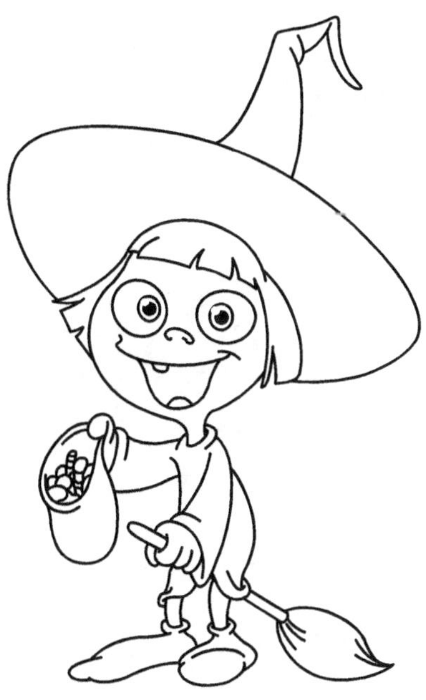

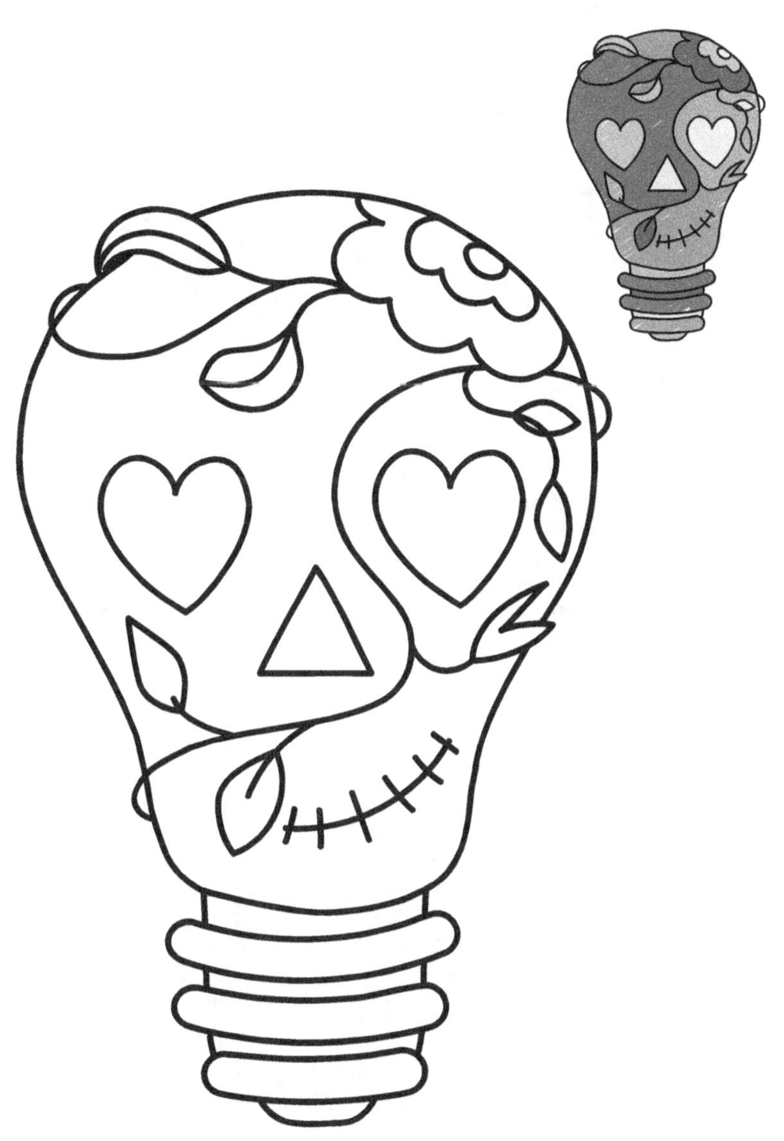

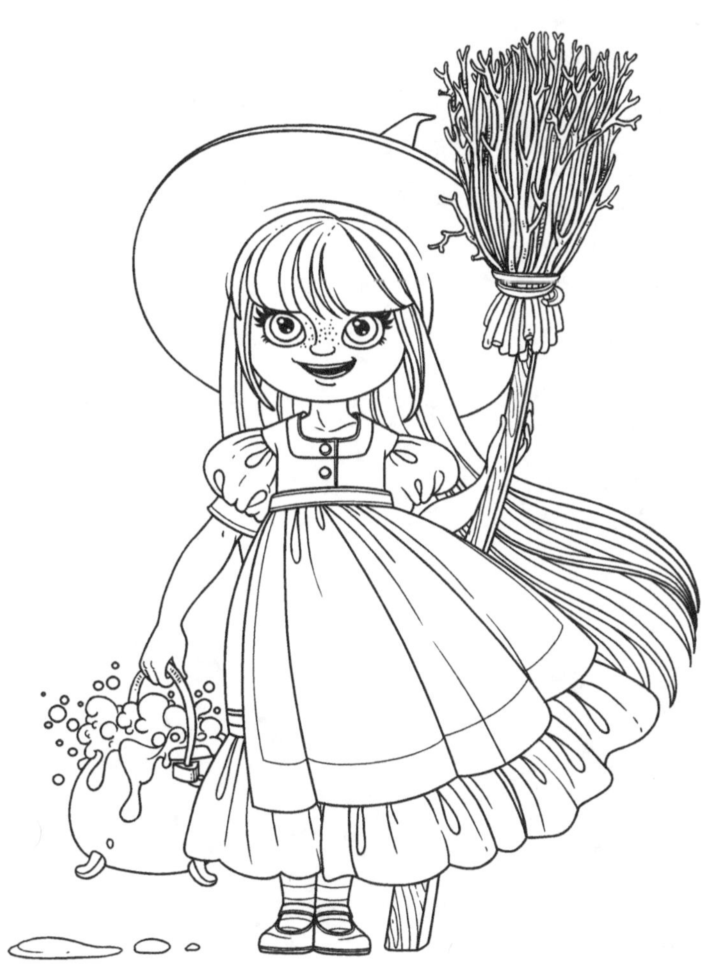

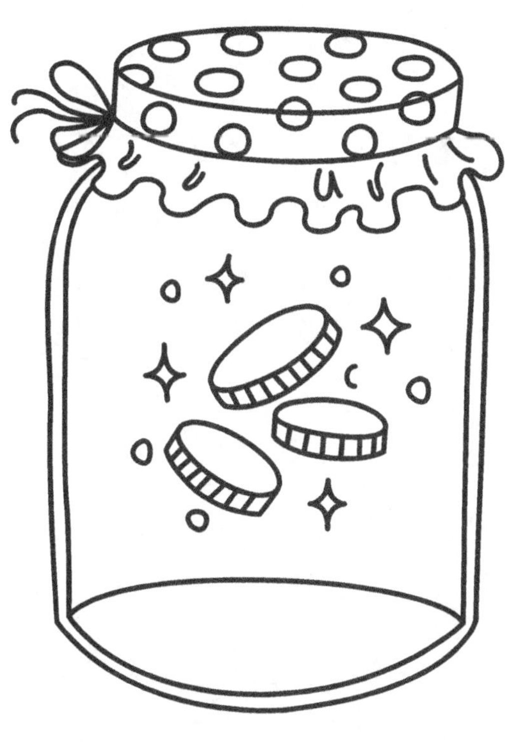

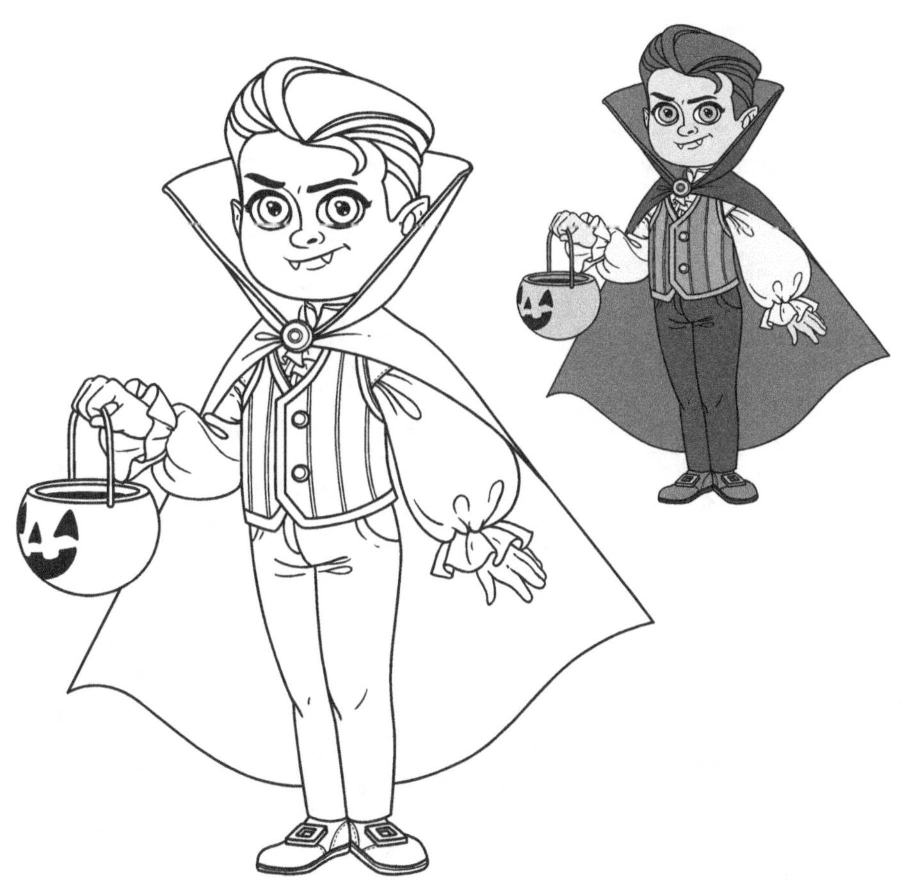

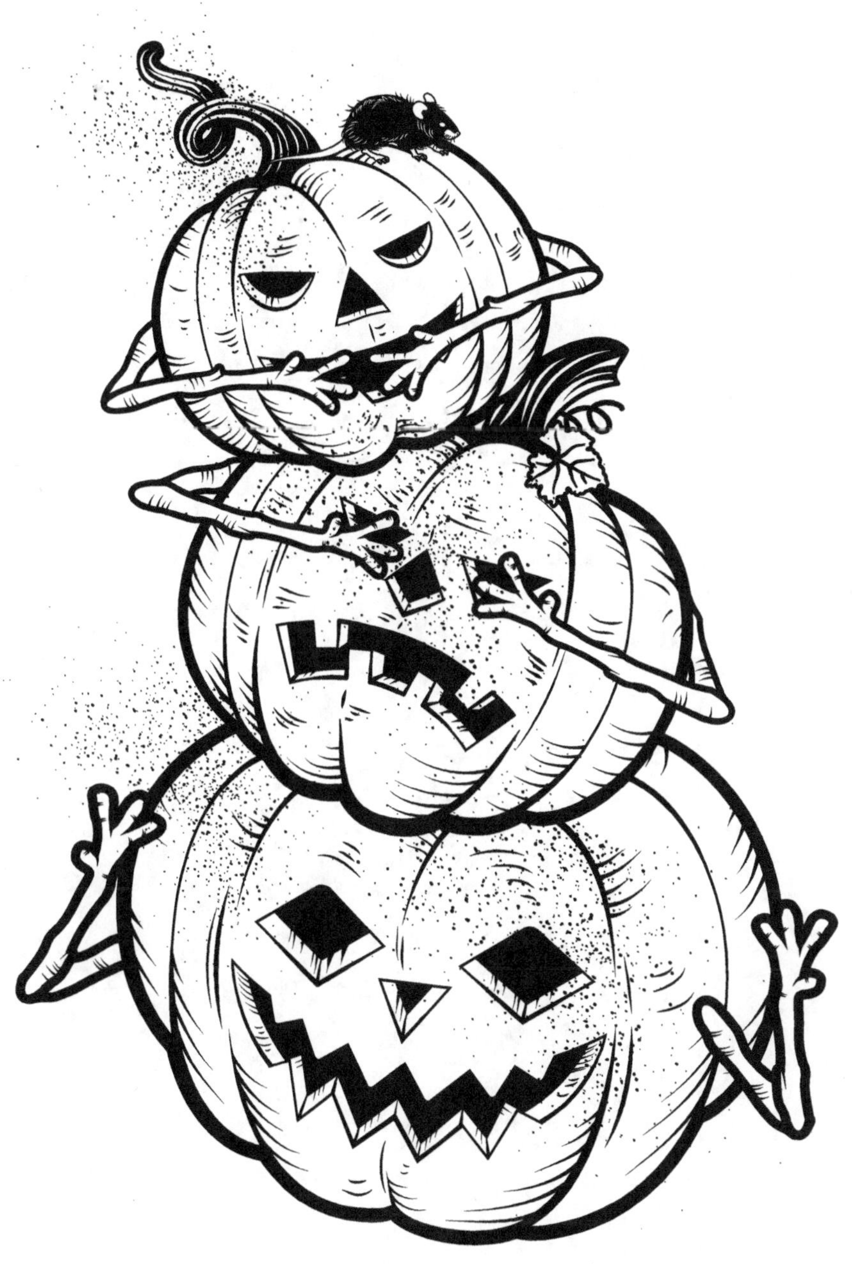

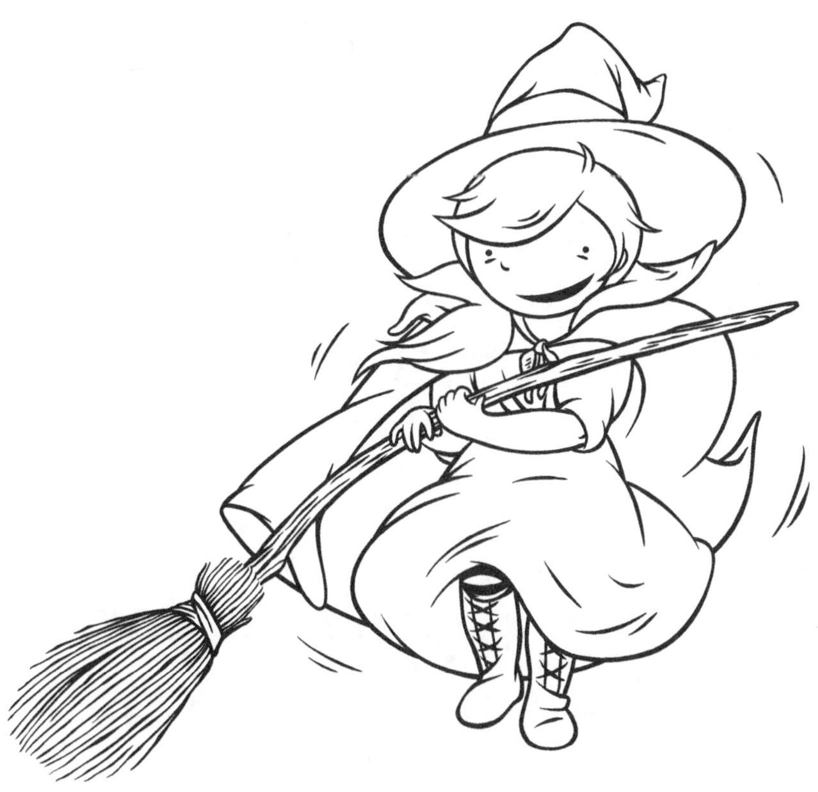

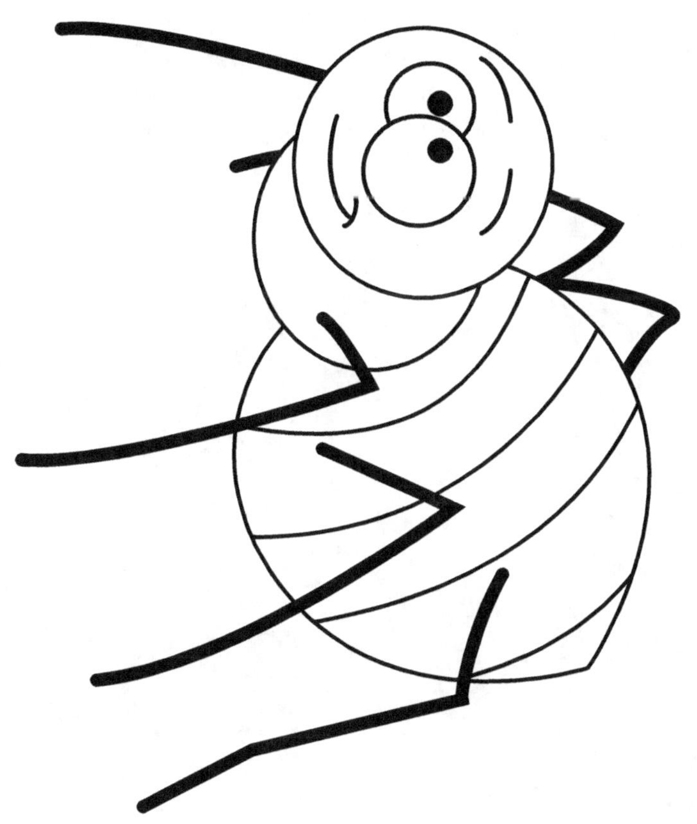

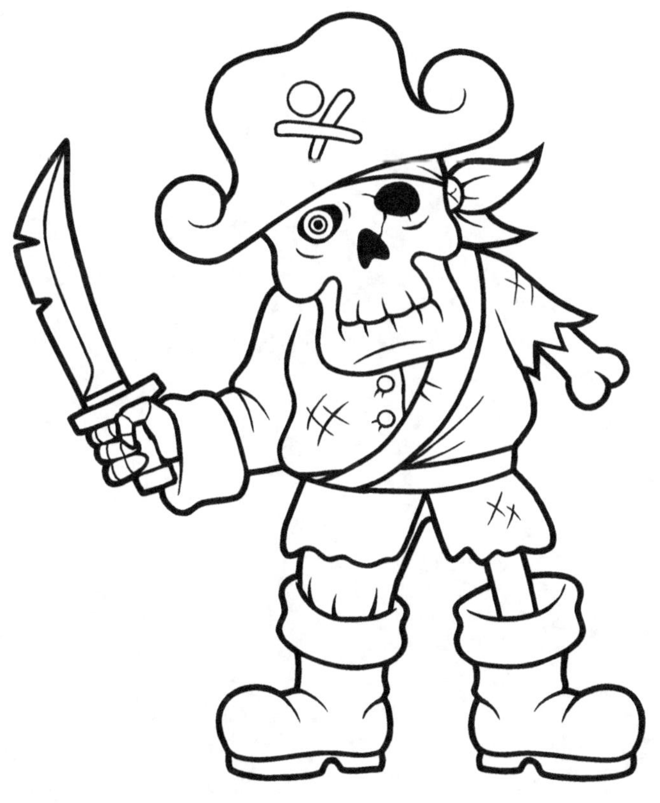

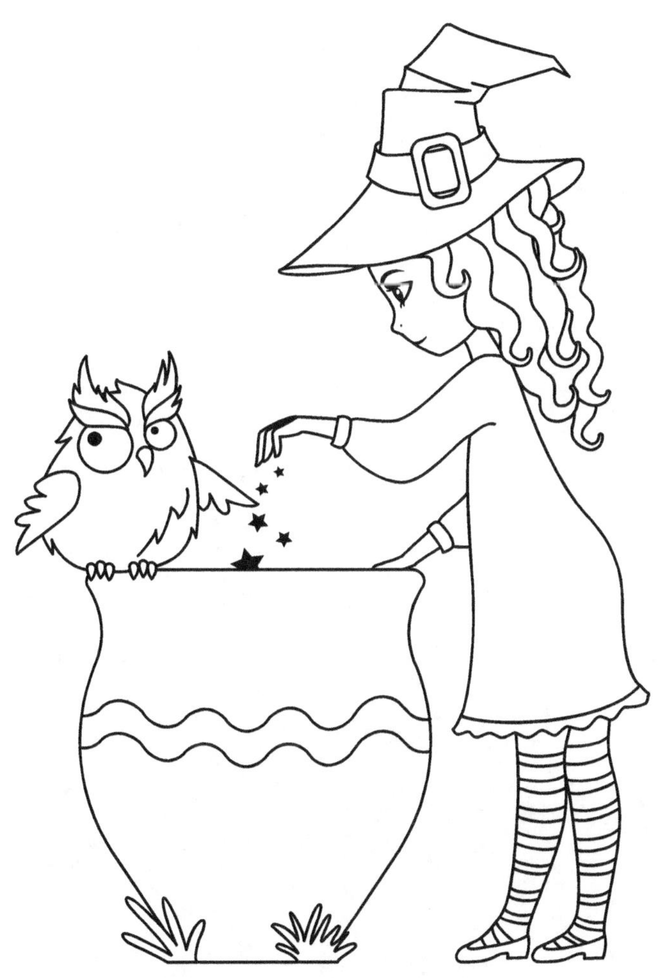

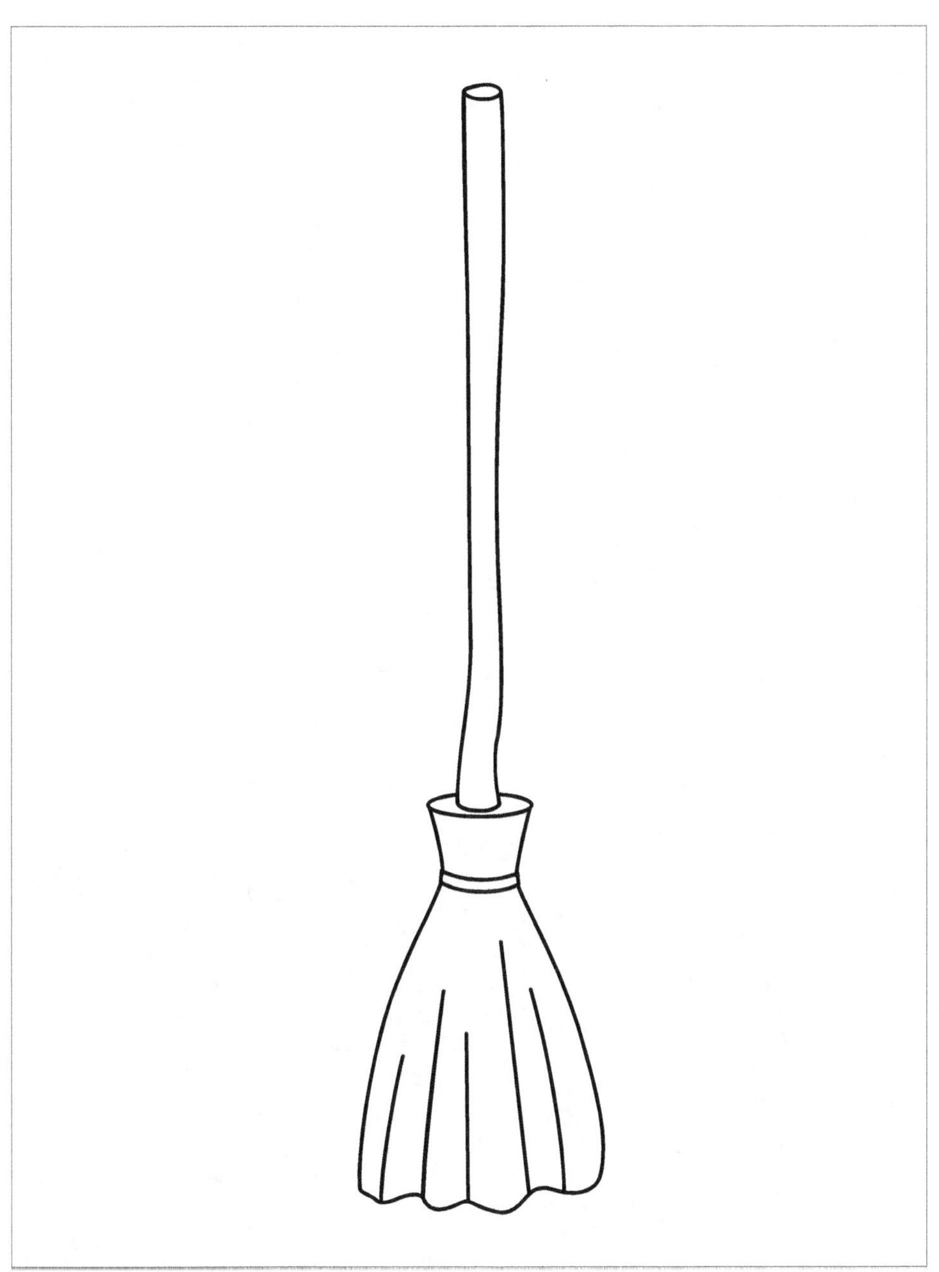

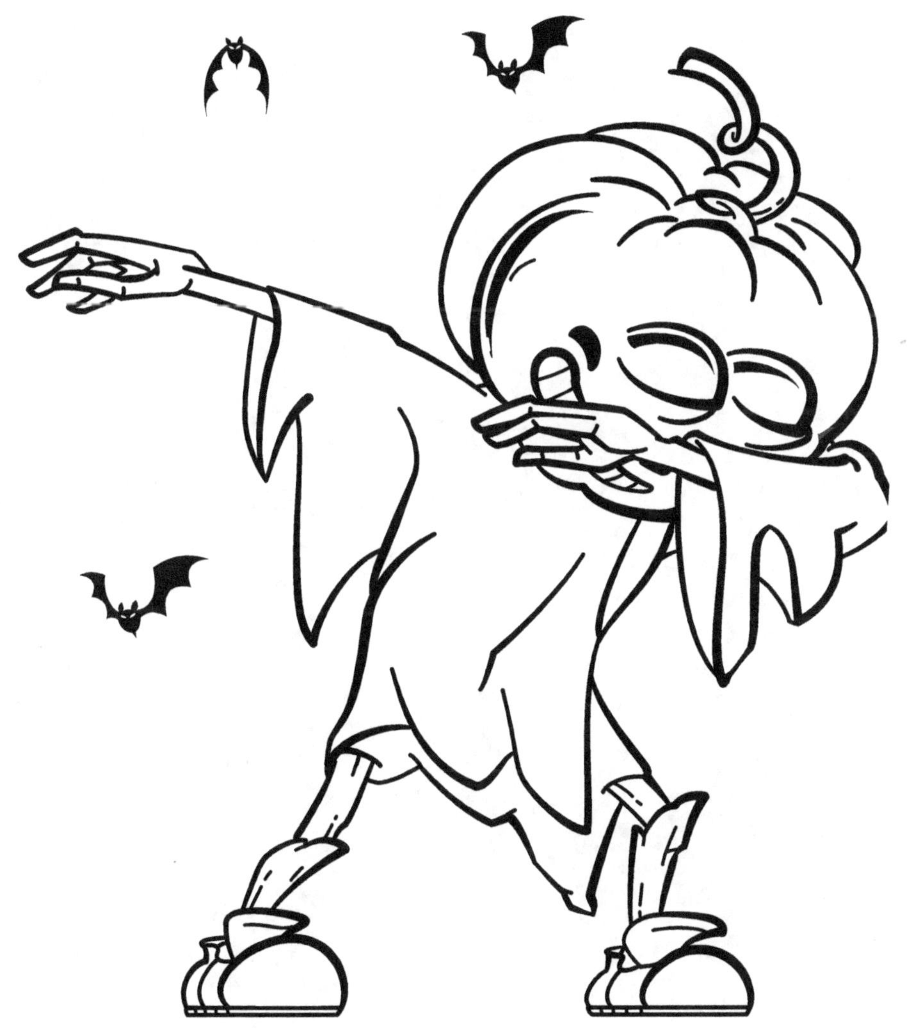

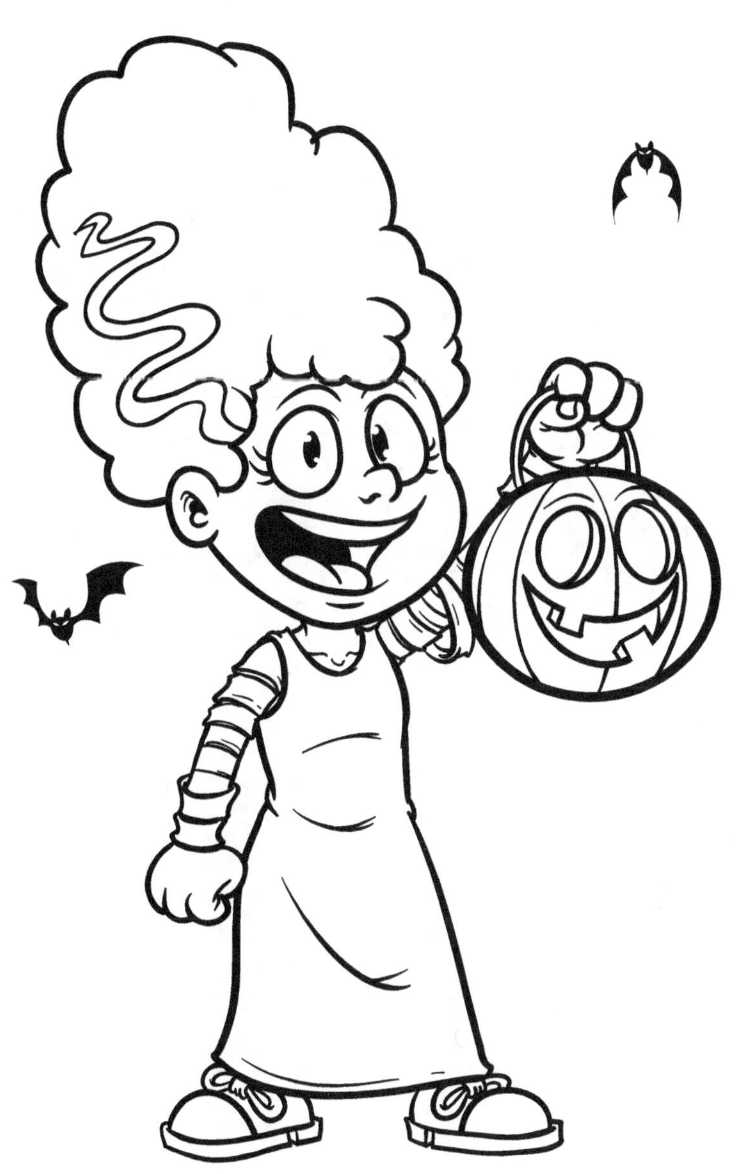

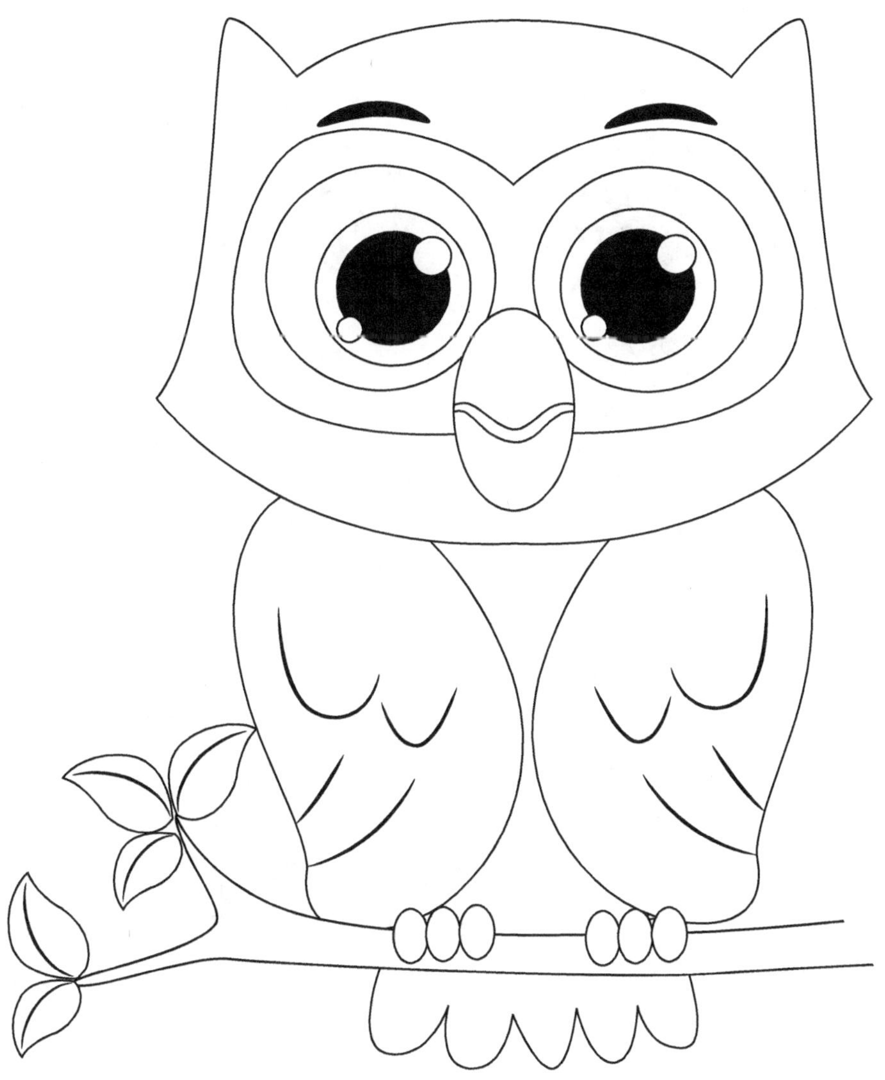

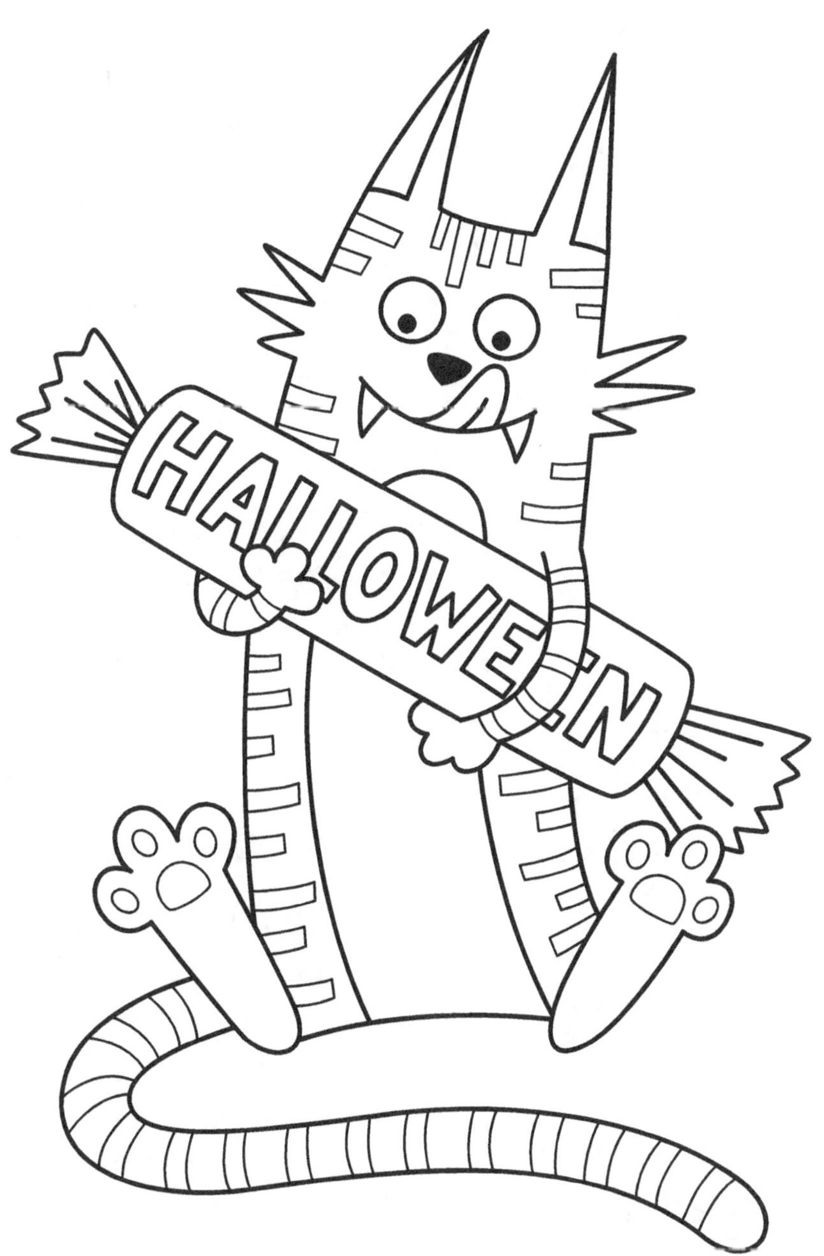

HALLOWE'N

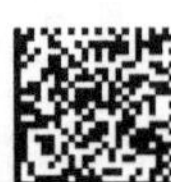

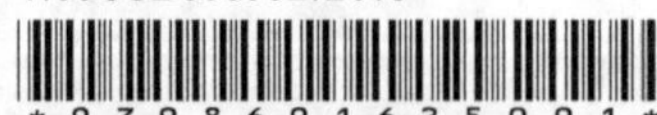

* 9 7 9 8 6 9 1 6 2 5 0 9 1 *